DEFENDING LENINGRAD

WOMEN BEHIND ENEMY LINES

By Kazimiera J. Cottam

Books

Bolesław Limanowski (1835-1935): A Study in Socialism and Nationalism, 1978

Soviet Airwomen in Combat in World War II, 1983

The Golden-Tressed Soldier, 1983 (Editor and Translator)

In the Sky Above the Front, 1984 (Editor and Translator)

The Girl from Kashin: Soviet Women in Resistance in World War II, 1984 (Editor and Translator)

On the Road to Stalingrad: Memoirs of a Woman Machine Gunner, 1997 (Editor and Translator)

Women in Air War: The Eastern Front of World War II, 1997 (Editor and Translator)

REVISED EDITION

DEFENDING LENINGRAD

WOMEN BEHIND ENEMY LINES

Edited and Translated by
Kazimiera J. Cottam

NEW MILITARY PUBLISHING
Nepean, Canada

Canadian Cataloguing in Publication Data

Main entry under title:

Defending Leningrad: women behind enemy lines

Rev. ed.
Translation of: *Devushka iz Kashina* and excerpts from *Ballada o krasnom desante and Taina Zoi Kruglovoi*. Published Manhattan, Kan.: MA/AH Pub., 1984 under title: The girl from Kashin.
Includes bibliographical references.
ISBN 0-9682702-3-9

    1. Konstantinova, Inessa Aleksandrovna, 1924-1944. 2. World War, 1939-1945 — Underground movements — Soviet Union. 3. World War, 1939-1945 — Women — Soviet Union. 4. World War, 1939-1945 — Personal narratives, Russian. I. Cottam, Kazimiera Janina, date. II. Title.

D802.R8D4913 1998	940.53'47	C98-900118-0

Printed and bound in Canada.

NEW MILITARY PUBLISHING
83-21 Midland Crescent
Nepean, ON K2H 8P6 Canada
Tel./Fax (613) 726-1596

CONTENTS

ILLUSTRATIONS

Fig. 1. Ina Konstantinova as a schoolgirl.

Fig. 2. Ina Konstantinova: a wartime snapshot.

Fig. 3. Ina's house on High Soviet Street in Kashin.

Fig. 4. Secondary School No. 1 in Kashin.

Fig. 5. Petr Ryndin, commander of 2nd Kalinin Partisan Brigade; Ina Konstantinova; and Ina's fellow partisans.

Fig. 6. Filipp Tyapin, detachment commander of 2nd Kalinin Partisan Brigade; and Ina's fellow partisans.

Fig. 7. Masha Poryvayeva and Georgiy Arbuzov.

Fig. 8. The pine-tree under which Ina was buried.

Fig. 9. The headstone on Ina's grave in Kashin.

Fig. 10. Masha Poryvayeva.

Fig. 11. Reunion at Masha Poryvayeva's School in Krasnoye.

Fig. 12. Agent Zoya Baiger.

ACKNOWLEDGEMENTS

This book is a second *revised* edition of a collection published in 1984 by MA/AH Publishing of Manhattan, Kansas, under the title *The Girl from Kashin: Soviet Women in Resistance in World War II.*

The principal sources of this collection are as follows: *Devushka iz Kashina* [The Girl From Kashin], ed. by G. Astaf'yev (Moscow: Moskovskiy Rabochiy, 1974) as well as *Tayna Zoi Kruglovoy* [The Secret of Zoya Kruglova] (Leningrad: Lenizdat, 1962) and *Ballada o krasnom desante* [A Ballad About the Red Airborne Assault Force] (Moscow: Politizdat, 1967), both by N.V. Masolov.

Excerpts from the first edition of this book have been published in *Children in the Holocaust and World War II: Their Secret Diaries*, ed. by Laurel Holliday (New York: Pocket Books, 1995).

Fig. 1-4 and 8-9 have been reproduced from *Devushka iz Kashina,* Fig. 5-7 from *Ballada o krasnom desante* and Fig. 10-12 from *Tayna Zoi Kruglovoy.* In addition to the illustrations reproduced from the above listed Soviet books, one photograph was obtained from I.N. Minayeva, *et al.*, eds., *Srazhalas za Rodinu. Pis'ma i dokumenty geroin' Velikoy Otechestvennoy voiny* [She Fought for the Homeland: Letters and Documents of Heroines of the Great Patriotic War] (Moscow: Mysl', 1964).

I wish to thank the former Copyright Agency of the USSR (VAAP) for permitting me to publish my translations of the copyrighted parts of this book and to reproduce the accompanying illustrations. I am also grateful to the staff of the Russian and East European Center as well as Slavic Reference librarians of the University of Illinois at Urbana-Champaign, for their assistance.

The research for this book has been subsidized by the Social Sciences and Humanities Research Council of Canada.

Kazimiera J. Cottam
Nepean, Canada

About one million women served in the Soviet Armed Forces during World War II, in diverse capacities, with the majority being at the front. By the end of 1943, women constituted about 8 percent of regular service personnel. While the same ratio applied to partisan women overall, women comprised 16 percent of the partisans in Belorussia. Around 27,000 women joined the partisan movement, and a great many were partisan scouts. By 1944, about 10 percent of women partisans were awarded military decorations, and those who received the title of Hero of the Soviet Union, the highest Soviet military award, numbered nearly thirty (constituting nearly one third of the total number of female recipients of the award).[1]

When Nazi Germany attacked the Soviet Union, the schoolgirl Ina Konstantinova was in her seventeenth year. She joined the partisans in the north-west of the Soviet Union at the age of eighteen, and was killed in combat about two years later, in March 1944, covering the retreat of her comrades.[2] In 1949 her remains were exhumed and transferred to a cemetery in her home town of Kashin.

Ina Konstantinova was born on 30 July 1924 in the village of Kiverichi, near the town of Kashin. She moved to Kashin with her family soon afterwards[3] and it was in this town, situated in Kalinin Region (formerly and currently Tver' Region), north-east of Moscow, that she spent her childhood and adolescence. Ina's parents were high school teachers; evidently, her father was also employed as a minor Party functionary, but it is not clear whether the administrative post he held was a part-time one and in addition to his teaching duties, or whether it eventually superseded his teaching.

Ina had a younger sister named Regina, who was to inherit the old, wooden single-family home in which the girls grew up. (Ina's mother and father died in 1958 and 1972 respectively.) The girls lived in fairly comfortable circumstances, and in their childhood were looked after by a nanny. Ina's family was apparently very close-knit and loving, and it was undoubtedly this that became a major source of her inner strength, enabling her to cope with the severe hardships she was to encounter in her service with the partisans, for which she was otherwise totally unprepared.

As a resistance heroine, Ina was far from unique, but it was her legacy, her letters and remarkable diary[4] that made her famous in the

ix

Soviet Union; her room had been transformed into a museum, her memory was cherished, and her life was being presented as an example for young people to follow. The diary, parts of which were written in a kind of poetic prose, reveals a highly sensitive young girl, with strong ties to her family, and an unusual sense of responsibility for her own destiny. Ina's diary begins in 1938, and consists of three distinct parts which cover three periods: the years before the war; the initial period of the war, before Ina joined the partisan movement; and Ina's life as a partisan. In the last period, Ina's letters at first alternate with and then replace her diary, which she eventually dispatched to her parents through a friend who had been wounded and was sent to a hospital in the rear. The originals of the diary and letters are property of her family; a copy of the diary was kept at the Komsomol's (Young Communist League) Central Committee Archives.

It seems that the initiative to publish Ina's letters and diary came from her parents. In 1947 the diary and letters were published by Molodaya Gvardiya, the Komsomol's publishing house, under the title: *Devushka iz Kashina* [The Girl From Kashin]. The book has since been reissued several times, in the Soviet Union as well as abroad. For instance, it had been translated into Bulgarian and French.

The book was translated into French by Elsa Triolet-Aragon, a prominent French writer born in Moscow, in 1897, who thus autographed a copy intended for Ina's parents: "To my dear Vera Vasil'yevna and Aleksandr Pavlovich, with tender love born of spiritual kinship. 28 March 1951. Elsa Triolet-Aragon." An excerpt from her letter to Ina's parents reads: "I became very fond of Ina while translating the book. I miss her as much as did those who knew her and those who were her kin."[5]

The latest Soviet edition, edited by G. Astaf'yev under the title *Devushka iz Kashina* and sub-titled *Dnevnik i pis'ma I. Konstantinovoy; vospominaniya i ocherki o ney* [The Girl From Kashin: The Diary and Letters of I. Konstantinova; Reminiscences and Sketches Concerning Her] was published by Moskovskiy Rabochiy Publishing House in 1974, on the 30th anniversary of her death. It included three biographical sketches, in addition to the somewhat abridged diary and letters. Further abridgements have been made here by the translator, particularly regarding parts of entries and entire entries, contributed by Ina before the German-Soviet war, and to avoid excessive repetitiveness.

The introductory biographical sketch of Part I, written by Olga Chechetkina, a Soviet journalist and author of other biographical sketches regarding prominent Soviet women, was published as an article in *Komsomol'skaya pravda*, the Komsomol's (Young Communist League's) main newspaper, in 1945. The final biographical sketch, by G. Astaf'yev and D. Petrov, had apparently been written especially for the 1974 edition; the former compiled the collection. It was reissued at a time when books pertaining to the war were being published in large quantities in the former USSR and were used for the purpose of "military-patriotic" education of youth.

However, my research into the operations of Soviet partisans in the rear of the German Army Group "North," that was blockading Leningrad, yielded no additional information on Ina's father — the author of Part III — who initially had been chief of intelligence of 2nd Kalinin Partisan Brigade and subsequently its deputy commander; in these capacities he was able to provide some first-hand information about Ina. The fact that she minimized the hardships she had experienced, so as not to worry her mother, is striking. Also, it is obvious that in her writing she avoided giving confidential information, striving to meet the requirements of wartime Soviet military censorship.

Thus, the sketch written by Ina's father after the war (between 1949 and 1972, the year of his death), successfully complements Ina's writings, filling the gaps in them to some extent and constituting a unique tribute to a brave daughter by a loving father.

Part II, "The Birch-Trees of Masha Poryvayeva," tells the story of Ina's friend and comrade-in-arms; it combines translations of selections from N.V. Masolov's *Ballada o krasnom desante* [A Ballad About the Red Airborne Assault Force] (Moscow: Politizdat, 1967) and his *Tayna Zoi Kruglovoy* [The Secret of Zoya Kruglova] (Leningrad: Lenizdat, 1962). A former teacher, war correspondent, and veteran of the Baltic Fleet, Nikolay Vissarionovich Masolov wrote about obscure heroes of the Battle for Leningrad.

Part III is a translation of one portion of the latter book by Masolov. The rationale for including in this book popular biographical sketches pertaining to Masha Poryvayeva and Zoya Kruglova was that they are in a sense complementary; in particular, this applies to Masha Poryvayeva's story. The three young girls (partisans Ina and Masha, and the army scout or secret agent Zoya) operated in roughly the same, strategically vital area, and all three made a contribution to Soviet victory in the north-west of the USSR.

Though their contributions were somewhat similar, interestingly the three young girls came from three divergent social backgrounds. Ina, a schoolgirl, was in a sense representative of small-town intelligentsia youth; Masha, a native of Moscow, came from the working class; and Zoya, a

Young Pioneer leader, was born and raised in a village, one of the daughters of a collective farm worker.

Kazimiera J. Cottam
Nepean, Canada

NOTES

1.   K. J. Cottam, "Soviet Women in Combat in World War II" (a series of articles): "The Ground Air Defense Forces," in Tova Yedlin, ed., *Women in Eastern Europe and the Soviet Union* (New York: Praeger Publishers, 1980), pp. 115-27; "The Ground Forces and the Navy," *International Journal of Women's Studies*, Vol. IV, No. 3 (July/August 1980), pp. 345-57; "The Rear Services, Resistance Behind Enemy Lines and Political Workers," *International Journal of Women's Studies*, Vol. V, No. 4 (September/October 1982), pp. 363-78.

2.   A number of women who fought in the Soviet Resistance movement and were killed left behind letters, short reminiscences, and inscriptions on jail walls, which are scattered in various collections, along with biographical data. See, for instance, Kondrat'yev, V.A. and Z.N. Politov, eds., *Govoryat pogibshiye geroi* [The Dead Heroes Speak], 8nd exp. and rev. ed. Moscow: Politizdat, 1986; Minayeva, I.N. *et al.*, eds., *Srazhalas' za Rodinu. Dokumenty i materialy geroin' Velikoy Otechestvennoy voiny* [She Fought for the Homeland: Documents and Materials of Heroines of the Great Patriotic War] Moscow: Mysl', 1964; and Ponomarenko, Yu.F. *et al.*, eds. *Molodaya gvardiya* [The Young Guard], 3rd rev. ed. Donetsk: Donbass, 1972.

3.   Minayeva, *et al.*, eds., *Srazhalas*, p. 10.

4.   A diary of another Soviet woman partisan, Nina Kosterina, was published in the United States. (In the Introduction, the translator compared it to the *Diary of Anne Frank*.) However, the diary ends prior to Kosterina's becoming a partisan. See *The Diary of Nina Kosterina*. Translated from the Russian. Introduction by Mirra Ginsburg. New York: Crown, 1969.

5.   G. Astaf'yev *et al.*, ed., *Devushka iz Kashina* (Moscow: Moskovskiy Rabochiy, 1974), p. 158.

PART I

SHE HAD A WONDERFUL YOUTH

Olga Chechetkina

The town of Kashin consists of a few low brick houses and many wooden ones. In the centre of the town there are rows of shops with long awnings; its bell towers are situated on hillocks; and a meandering stream with steep, precipitous banks encircles the town like a silvery belt.

On a snow-covered Kashin street, in a little house with yellow shutters, there lived Inessa Konstantinova, a Russian girl who sacrificed her life for her country.

Ina was a simple, ordinary Soviet schoolgirl, who was experiencing the best time of her life: her youth. Her devoted parents, Aleksandr Pavlovich and Vera Vasil'yevna, had two daughters — Ina and her sister Rena. Wise and tactful pedagogues, they not only imparted theoretical knowledge to their children but also taught them how to live. Kashin is not too distant from Moscow, so the parents made sure that their girls were exposed to the culture of the capital.

Ina loved reading and frequented all the libraries in Kashin. Her love of literature led her to the home of the photographer Kolotil'shchikov, an old resident of Kashin. Here hundreds of photographs, taken over a period of more than fifty years, told the story of her home town.

Often, in the evening, she would say to her girlfriend Lyusya: "Let's climb the snowdrifts!" Together, they explored the town's dark and narrow streets, sinking into the snow with an infectious giggle, breathing the clean, frosty air, or suddenly stopping and saying: "Let's look at the stars," and dreaming....

On a clear and bright June day, Ina was walking along the edge of a precipice with her boyfriend. She knew that he loved her, she believed him, and all the same she said: "Mishka, you don't love me...."

"I don't love you? You want me to prove that I do?"

Presto! Misha jumped from the precipice.

She came home with a huge branch, broken off by Misha while he was making his "fatal jump." Her mother was angry and grumbled: "Well, what's the point of bringing this thing here?" But Ina believed the branch was her talisman, a guarantee of happiness.

* * *

The first train with wounded soldiers arrived in Kashin. Ina, along with other girls, had waited for the train all night. And when the wounded were being carried out of the hospital cars, she caught her first glimpse of the war. Ina tended the wounded soldiers with all the love and kindness her tender heart could muster. She spent her days at school and her nights in the hospital; this was her new life.

On a sunny day, when the sky was intensely blue, Ina came face-to-face with death. A wounded man lay beside a window; light green birch-tree branches peeped into the room. The wounded man said: "What a beautiful day...." And then he died.

Ina cried all night. And when she began to feel too confined in Kashin, working in the hospital, she applied to a recruitment centre asking to be inducted into the field forces of the Red Army.

She waited for an answer.

At night troops marched in the streets of Kashin. Ina listened to the voices, the dull sound of the footsteps, and the clinking of weapons. She wondered: "When will the answer come?"

Ina was intent on realizing her dream. And then she learned that her father was about to join a partisan detachment. When Vera Vasil'yevna, her mother, told her: "Why should you go to the front — stay in the hospital," Ina replied: "Mom, this is not what you have been telling me in the classroom." So the mother was silenced.

And then came her last day at home. What were her thoughts that day? In the morning she wandered in the nearby forest, and she came back with a large bouquet of lilies of the valley. She was very fond of them: of the snow-white purity of the flower, the even, glossy green of the leaves, and of the narcotizing aroma.

In the evening, Ina went to her graduation. Rushing to school, she ran along a small ravine, all dressed up, merry, and radiant from happiness and the rays of the setting sun. The next day, Ina left Kashin.

The girl from Kashin became a brave partisan. She crossed the front lines several times, and then stayed behind enemy lines. A partisan scout worked very hard and faced mortal danger every day; Ina Konstantinova gathered intelligence for nearly two years.

While gathering intelligence, fighting, and living the life of a partisan behind enemy lines, Ina was reunited with her father, Aleksandr Pavlovich [who was chief of intelligence and subsequently deputy commander of a partisan brigade]. Ina worshipped her father. She liked to look at his grey head when he worked out an itinerary, bent over a map. They sustained each other with their mutual affection. She worried a lot when she was separated from him and didn't know what fate had befallen him. To make up for it, their reunions were tremendously joyful.

Ina frequently wrote lengthy letters home. Now that she was experiencing the hardships and dangers of a soldier's life, her home, mother and sister, became even closer and dearer to her than before.

On 4 March 1944, Ina with a group of scouts went on a mission. In a forest, they were to meet another group of partisans in a hidden dugout. Ina walked in a snow-covered, moonlit white forest. And, who knows, perhaps she recalled what she had once written in her diary:

> The moon.... Everything is so beautiful, like in a fairy tale.... I do love moonlit nights so! Then the world becomes purer, better, and the blue light bewitches everything with its magic.... And the silence, the silence.... Just as in a fairy tale! On such a night, you want to think about something wonderful and impossible.... Some day, on such a night, I'll go into the forest. And the fairy tale will come to pass.... [13 December 1940]

Perhaps that night, too, the girl from Kashin dreamed her fairy tale. The fairy tale did come to pass. It was a tale about her immortality, and the way to attain it was heroism.

At dawn, a detachment of German soldiers followed the scouts' tracks and surrounded their dugout; the scouts realized they were trapped. And then Ina ordered her comrades to go away, while she stayed behind to engage the enemy; she covered the scouts' retreat with her submachine gun. When the next day the partisans returned to their dugout, they found Ina nearby, dead. They buried her in the woods under a tall, fluffy pine.

Ina's spotlessly clean, tiny room had been transformed into a museum to keep her memory alive. In this small, white room of a young girl, the frost has fashioned clever flowery patterns on the windows, and a bouquet of lilies of the valley stands in a vase on a shelf. It has not withered but merely dried up. The leaves are no longer green but pale grey; yet, they are still carefully supporting the tiny capitula of the flowers. These are the same lilies of the valley that Ina had gathered during her last day at home, her last day as a civilian.

Komsomol'skaya pravda, 8 March 1945

(School Years: 1940-1942)

7 March 1940

I finished reading *Les Misérables*, by Victor Hugo. The book made a tremendous impression on me. Truly, these people were social outcasts.[1] Reading this book, you can feel the author's compassion, his true love for his heroes. And the reader also loves them. I cried for a long time, after I had read about Jean Valjean's death. What a noble, pure spirit this convict was! Upholding fame and fortune of other people, he sacrificed himself and his own well-being.... But those for whom he sacrificed himself, particularly Cosette, I don't like. She was too egoistic. How could she forget the one who was her surrogate father for so long, so easily! She was oblivious to everything but her happiness.

10 July 1940

What a wonderful, cool evening! Under my windows gilly-flowers bloom; the air is full of their aroma. Everything is so perfect, so quiet. But, in spite of the delightful evening, something is missing. I long for something supernatural, unusual, something that would turn my life into a beautiful fairy tale.

Ethereal day-dreams, light reveries come to me. About happiness, life, him.... Yes, mainly about him. I shall soon be sixteen. At my age it is natural to think such thoughts. Is there anything wrong in wanting to love? After all, it is a pure, holy, and beautiful sentiment. Perhaps I haven't yet really experienced it.... Perhaps what has happened was a mere presentiment of love, its vision. Well, what of it! It means that it will eventually come. I am waiting....

ON THE LAST DAY OF MY CHILDHOOD

29 July 1940

It is painful to give up all that is close and dear to us, especially one's childhood. This is the morning of our lives....

We associate our best memories with it. Today I am still a little girl and tomorrow I'll be a young woman. How sad! How swiftly the marvellous, unforgettable years have passed, which (alas!) will never, never, return. I stand on the threshold of adulthood: my entire youth will pass just as imperceptibly as my childhood did. And then I'll face...life! What will the future bring me?

I am convinced: the pure, radiant joys of childhood are gone forever. Good-bye, my morning. My day, bright but exhausting, has begun. And there, at the end, my old age awaits me. But will I reach it? Better not to experience this evening of life at all. For it brings...death.

Good-bye, childhood, forever.

5 October 1940

... Chaykovskiy's *Yevgeniy Onegin* is now being broadcasted; Lenskiy is singing his celebrated "What has the future in store for me?" This tune is well-suited to day-dreaming, day dreaming about something sad, sorrowful, and yet immeasurably beautiful. I am listening to the radio and am close to tears....

24 October 1940

I received my first passport.

7 November 1940

I feel like lying down somewhere, by myself, to think. Not about the present, but about the future, about something bright and wonderful!

And the present.... My grades are poor: I got two "satisfactory" marks in the past quarter. One of my girlfriends, the one dearest to me, went away. I feel so painfully alone, so lost in this huge universe. My present, impetuous life is passing me by, as it were; I have to overcome so many difficulties. Sometimes it seems to me that'll never gain control over my own life; this causes me such anguish. I have to act in a way so as to ensure that I am in charge of my life and not vice versa. Only then I'll have the right to call myself a human being.

I remember a saying that I've heard somewhere, and which I've involuntarily memorized forever: "Only that individual who has earned his niche in history [truly] has the right to life." Perhaps it is so....

9 November 1940

Yesterday we attended festivities at the children's home, which exceeded all my expectations.... I came home at 2:00 a.m.

And even today the impressions of yesterday's evening are so vivid.... What a good time I've had.... There were such dear, nice people all around me; all merry, smiling, friendly. I love them all, all the kids in this children's home, as if they were my dearest brothers and sisters. I would love so to live among them, with them! I simply didn't want to leave. It seems to me that I have known them all for a long, long time.

16 November 1940

Beauty is the most important thing in life, for it makes life happy. Is it possible for sorrow to coexist with beauty? Regardless of how it is expressed: beauty physical, spiritual; beautiful dreams, beautiful sentiments.... Only a noble individual comprehends beauty; and bows down before it. Such were my sentiments after viewing *The Great Waltz*.

4-5 December 1940

... I don't know what is the matter with me; now I enjoy life and want to do something exciting, and now I suddenly begin to pine away and become apathetic and indifferent toward everything.

13 December 1940

The moon.... Everything is so beautiful, like in a fairy tale.... I do love moonlit nights so. Then the world becomes purer, better, and the blue light bewitches everything with its magic. It is very cold. The snow sparkles in a silvery light. And the silence, the silence.... Just as in a fairy tale!

On such a night, you want to think about something wonderful and impossible. The very surroundings favour such a mood. Some day, on such a night I'll go into a forest. And the fairy tale will come to pass....

I'll enter an enchanted world, full of miraculous surprises. Silvery, blue light.... Can there be anything more beautiful?

People are born, live, love, suffer, and die. Death ends everything. Death is the end. And even this great, unavoidable mystery becomes less alien and more comprehensible to you during such a magic, fantastic night....

4 March 1941

Uncle Kostya paid us a visit today; he is on leave from the army. He was on the Finnish front, in Western Belorussia, and Estonia. He had a great deal to say.

12 March 1941

I've just finished reading Lev Kassil's book, entitled *Mayakovskiy*

Himself. If only I could find words to express my emotional state; I cried over this book. What a fine person this big, complicated man was! What a kind, warm soul he had!

How helpless and sensitive this man was! When you read the book, he comes to life before your eyes, standing upright and so tall, and you love him, love him as one can only love the best among men. How touching his hurts and vexations were, and how his smiles gladdened!

Handsome, strong, deep-breathing, he was an individual so complete and unique, in terms of his entire presence, that there couldn't have been another human being like him in the past and couldn't be in the future.

> In other people the heart is housed
> In the chest, a well-known fact!
> But in me
> The anatomy has gone berserk.
> A continuous heart
> Is beating everywhere....

This is how Kassil describes his death (I simply would have liked to cite the entire book here):

"Mayakovskiy was like a factory manufacturing happiness, not knowing standstills or days off. He inexcusably overextended himself. Then came the 'most terrible kind of wear and tear, the wear and tear of heart and soul....' A minor misunderstanding with friends, a temporary absence of the people closest to him, condemned him to solitude. And a coincidental small personal misfortune, which normally would have merely shaken him up, now threw him of his rails at full speed.

"And the notion of death is so incompatible with our image of the frenzied poet, that, when you enter the lobby of the Mayakovskaya Station of the Moscow Metro, everything seem possible and believable: at any moment, the escalator — steep, stepped, and running just like Mayakovskiy's line — will raise the familiar, broad-shouldered figure from the platform; and the creature, banging with his walking stick, will begin to stride across life firmly and energetically: Vladimir Mayakovskiy, not of the past but all contemporary, all future-orientated, and [ours] forever."

16 April 1941

Spring, spring has sprang, a very real spring. Wonderful! Well, is it possible to describe all the sudden sensations experienced during joyful moments such as these?

Well... I am in a most spring-like mood. I am experiencing a sensation of freshness, happiness, lightness, and a kind of happy and tender sadness. I wait and hope for something to happen and I believe in a tremendous, real happiness. The air is so pure, gay, and so impossibly fresh....

22 April 1941

Here is spring for you! There is snow all around; a great deal of it has fallen. The trees are completely white, everything is white; you would think we were in November!

Last night I finished reading Jack London's *Martin Eden*. This book made a strong impression on me; it has shaken me up! So Martin has now become one of my best loved heroes. What fine person he was, how bright! You can't forget him or confuse him with anyone else. How I cried at the end, and even before the end! I had already then come to know him. Could this giant's fate been different in such conditions? Of course, not. He stood immeasurably above all of his entourage. He could not find an equal among members of the upper class in intellect, power of thought, and understanding of life, and he could no longer return to his milieu; he died suffocated by loneliness. It was not Ruth who happened to be the cause of his decline, for one cannot help but so define the period of his life characterized by a single refrain: "My work is finished!" when apathy and indifference toward everything took over. Ruth was the cause of only the initial push backward, and then everything came down of its own accord. Martin kept climbing the high tower of happiness with such stubbornness, and with such difficulty. Yet, when he had almost reached the top, he suddenly began to slide down and in the end perished at the bottom.

And, as for Ruth, you couldn't call her a nonentity.... Obviously, she was a mediocrity and nothing more. Lizzie Connolly was depicted as being more sympathetic, a better person, and more beautiful. At least she could truly love. All in all, an amazing book.

6 May 1941

Well, the holidays ended long ago. I had a good time. Only I was saddened by the absence of Lyusya. Otherwise, I had such fun!

We were already dreaming about another such party, in about seven to ten years. Oh, we were so carried away by our dreams! I couldn't even recognize our group. All were so excited, their eyes shining, cheeks flashed — so much joy generated by a mere anticipation of a future reunion. What will we be like then? And above all, would it happen? More likely, it wouldn't, but we were such dreamers, we believed so in our dream....

Yesterday, I re-read (for the umpteenth time!) the book entitled *Gadfly*, by Voynich. And I cried over it even more than before.

17 June 1941

Yesterday we had a party for the tenth-graders at school. It was their graduation dance. We were also invited, but we arrived late. On our way there, we walked along the town's edge. The evening was fabulous, and we all held black-alder flowers; the air was literally full of their aroma. We were in a glorious mood; everything pleased us, everything caused us joy. We danced to a brass band.

* * *

22 June 1941

Only yesterday everything was so peaceful, so quiet, and to-day...my God!

At noon we heard Molotov's speech broadcasted over the radio: Germany is bombing our nation, and bombs have fallen on Kiev, Zhitomir, and other Ukrainian cities. The country is endangered. I can't describe my state of mind as I listened to this speech! I became so agitated that my heart seemed about to jump out. The country is mobilizing; could I continue as before? No! I ought to make myself useful to my homeland in its hour of need, to the best of my ability. We must win the war!

23 June 1941

This is the second day of the war. Only the second day, but these two days were more eventful that the past two years. Our region was placed under martial law, meaning that on the streets lights are forbidden after 10:00 p.m. General mobilization has been declared. Our boys have already been called up; soon they will go away.

Daddy has already been mobilized, too, but he is still in Kashin. And what about me? If only there was a way of making myself useful at the front! Immediately, without any hesitation, I would then volunteer for service in the war zone. But...what could I do there now? Well, nothing. But my turn will come, too.

* * *

Fig. 1. Ina Konstantinova
as a schoolgirl.

Fig. 2. Ina Konstantinova:
a wartime snapshot.

Fig. 3. The house on High Soviet Street in Kashin, where Ina spent her childhood and adolescence.

Fig. 4. Secondary School No. 1 in Kashin, which Ina attended.

3 July 1941

Oh, what a night we had today! I'll never, never forget it. I'll start at the beginning. A week ago, I joined a voluntary aid detachment. We train every day from seven to ten. Yesterday some of us were summoned for duty to the District Committee of the Red Cross. The time was 10:30 p.m. We were issued night passes, bandages, respirators, and medical bags. Then we were sent to the Technical School. Here everything was made ready to receive a trainload of wounded soldiers. Covered trucks and buses stood by; we climbed into them. I found myself among the Technical School kids.

We sat up all night, until 4:00 a.m. Finally, we drove to the train station. The train arrived at 5:30 a.m., and the unloading began. What an experience! I'll never forget the face of an agitated woman, accompanying the wounded, who, with tears in her eyes, almost threw her arms around my neck and kept repeating joyfully: "My dear girl, have we really arrived? It is so good to see you!"

I'll never forget the blue eyes of a soldier, a mere youngster, semi-closed and suddenly opening up and flashing from an unbearable pain. How he suffered! I'll never forget this dark-haired youth with both legs torn off.

We carried and transported these people, and gave them directions.... But what I remember best was the mood of the soldiers. They all believed in victory; all were cheerful. We transported a girl soldier, a Latvian, wounded in one leg. She spoke almost no Russian. There were many wounded civilians, too, mainly from Riga. No, I could never fully describe what I lived through that night. In the morning I was completely tired out. But it didn't matter!

5 July 1941

We are having a storm.... And what a storm! Lightning flashes every second, and it is raining so hard you can't see anything outside the windows. The thunder is deafening.

But the country is in the throes of a storm which is a hundred times more terrible!

16 July 1941

A terrible misfortune has befallen this country. The Germans are already so near.... They are bombing Leningrad, Mozhaysk. They are advancing toward Moscow....

We are training in a voluntary aid detachment, and are working in a hospital.

How troubled our life has become! There is an airfield near Kashin; aircraft take off from it constantly. Military detachments march along the streets. Field units, anti-aircraft guns, and tanks have arrived.

Even the atmosphere has changed somehow. What does the future hold in store for us? I am anxious to finish training, and...to go to the front. I dream of...Nazi defeat, of defending our country and making us happy again!

29 July 1941

What dreadful times we live in! Yesterday evening we heard the familiar phrase on radio: "Citizens, this is an air-raid warning!"

The alert was not the first, but it was the first night alert. We dashed to the assembly point as usual, to the recruitment office. At first it was quiet, but then.... All night long we heard aircraft engines' roar and the rumble of remote explosions. We saw the flashes of anti-aircraft gunfire and the lightning-like explosions. There was fighting going on somewhere nearby. How dreadful! Moscow is being bombed regularly for some time now. When will this nightmare end?

Our medical training is over. We passed the examinations, and I received "excellent" marks. We were issued uniforms. How I wish we were going to the war zone! Daddy says that I should be mindful of other people's needs. I should ask myself: "How can I make myself useful to them?" I pondered over what he said. Yes, I am bound to make myself useful to my country, somehow. That's what really matters!

5 August 1941

On 30 July I turned seventeen. A year ago I had no idea what lay ahead. And what lies ahead for me a year from now? If the war had not yet ended by then, I'll definitely enlist. I am bound to be accepted by then. Indeed, by then I would already be eighteen.

Every night Moscow is subjected to air raids. The enemy troops are coming closer and closer. How awful! Never mind, they'll soon be stopped. How tenaciously our soldiers do repel the wily enemy's attacks! I can't help being excited about the feat of Captain Gastello. What a hero! His aircraft caught fire in flight. He then directed his plane onto enemy fuel storage tanks and was killed in the ensuing explosion. And there are many such Gastellos, Pavlovs, and other famous people. Such heroes are bound to save our homeland. We must save it!

17 August 1941

Yesterday a Komsomol [Young Communist League] working Sunday was observed throughout the Union. We were working on a collective farm. All day long we hauled flax; I was tired but contented at the end of the day.

26 August 1941

Again, I am working at the hospital — every day, from 6:00 a.m. to 6:00 p.m., and I get so tired. I am on duty in the isolation ward. School will resume on 1 October.

4 October 1941

I haven't written for so long!

I have just returned from the forest, from taking part in a successful logging operation. On 1 October we went to school. The day before we had transported a group of wounded all night, and so we went to school in the morning without any sleep.

When we were assembled, we were informed that school will begin on the 6th, and in the meantime the girls would work on collective farms, while the boys were assigned to logging operations. This year, there are a great many new people in school, all refugees, the majority of them from Moscow and Leningrad.

We girls asked the director to let us go to the woods. The forest was located near the village where Klara Kalinina's grandmother lives. It was very beautiful there. We started sawing; on the first day everyone worked fairly well.

The second day was successful, too, but in the evening we went back to Kashin. The next morning we returned to the woods. Indeed, these two days were the greatest. The boys organized the teams. One such "team" comprised: Yura; Sasha, a new pupil from Moscow; Zhenya Nikiforov, whom we christened "Byron" because of his looks, also a Muscovite; and Rem Men'shikov from Leningrad. All were wonderful, really nice kids; they invited Klara and me to work with them. We were delighted. The kids were working remarkably well; the chips were flying high. Before noon we cut more than 10 cubic metres, while the norm was nine.

6 October 1941

Well, finally, I am in Grade 10. We are seniors! For some reason, today seems to have already happened long, long ago.

What is there to report about yesterday?... In the morning I sat down to write a letter to Lyusya. Suddenly, I heard an air-raid warning. I stopped writing in the middle of a word and dashed to the assembly point.

After all-clear was sounded, we were told to go back to our hospital duty. I went to the isolation ward about 6:00 p.m. There were only three patients and all were recovering. One of them, Zaslavskiy, a native of Rostov, an interesting young man wounded in one leg, shoulder, and head, asked me to write several letters for him. That evening, I wrote four letters.... If all were like him, the barbarians' stay on our territory would have been cut short.

We talked for a long time, then the light went out and he fell asleep. I went out into the corridor, sat there for a while, and then wandered a bit. The night dragged on and on. It was terribly cold. Sleep was out of the question! I got home in the morning. I've hardly slept and it was already time to go to school.

I arrived in school ten minutes before the bell. Our classroom is located in the corner, in the upper storey. It is small, comfortless, cold.... It's too early to tell, but it seems to be an unfriendly class. We'll see.

The lessons passed quickly. Directly after school, I dropped on Dad, into the District [Party] Committee, to pick up a history textbook. I walked there with Yu. and Sasha. On the way, Sasha told me that he likes my personality; he considers me strong-willed. How thoroughly mistaken he is! On the contrary, my personality is unattractive and unpleasant. But he called himself a morally weak person. I certainly don't agree. Well, I better end this; it's growing dark. Days are short now; fall is here.

9 October 1941

We have been attending school for four days already. How good it is to go to school, to study, to fearfully anticipate being questioned, and to rejoice when all goes well.

Nothing new happened at school today. Actually, that's not true. During the second lesson, I glanced through the window: everyone was running, rushing about.... It was an air-raid warning! We ran to the first aid station, and the rest into the shelter. Twenty minutes later, "all clear" was sounded. We returned to school.

Today, an announcement was made over the radio that Orel had fallen. One more city gone: additional thousands without a roof over their heads, sleeping under an open sky; thousands tormented to death, tortured....

The enemy troops have occupied so much territory that it would take a long time for life to return to normal after their expulsion.

Perhaps we were not meant to live peacefully and undisturbed. This is no time for living a private life. Everyone should serve the country! And indeed many years from now people will study the history of our times and will envy us. Without a doubt, we are living in glorious times, full of heroism and valour. All private concerns have been pushed aside, for they are now less important than the nation's well-being.

10 October 1941

Already five days have passed since we began attending school. This whole year will fly by just as fast, if only we are allowed to complete it. Again, today we heard an air-raid warning. Two German aircraft circled above the town; having accomplished nothing, they flew home. Our boys climbed onto the roof, and we ran to our first-aid station.

There were no calls for me so far.

This month our school will give a concert in the hospital. David will sing, and Zhenechka and Klara will both recite. I don't know yet what else has been prepared.

14 October 1941

Again we have interrupted school. Most of the pupils were sent to a collective farm for four days. The first-aiders, however, were left behind in town, to cope with air-raid warnings. The detachment was on duty in the hospital, where many patients were recovering from their wounds.

What a good feeling it is to observe a person who was brought to you barely alive gradually getting better, becoming more cheerful, talking, smiling, and then standing up and walking. Indeed, it is sheer happiness to be able to put someone on his feet, and to restore him to full health!

Yesterday Zaslavskiy took a walk to the window and back. Pichugin also tried to walk. How wonderful! I drop on them very often; they now look forward to my visits and keep asking the nurses when I am expected to come.

I am going back to school tomorrow. I am looking forward to seeing the kids again, since I've already begun to miss them a bit.

15 October 1941

Yesterday I came home to find a heap of things in the kitchen. Two refugees from Kalinin arrived to stay with us: a woman teacher and her little daughter.

Daddy went away today; he travels through the district preparing the people for evacuation. This means that we, too, are about to leave Kashin. But how? And what would our destination be? Nobody knows. Perhaps we'll be evacuated in the same manner as these people from Kalinin were? This would not be too bad. But what if we are compelled to leave on foot? Well, where could we go on foot?

What an awful news item! The entire Kalinin lies in ruins; the Germans will occupy it any day.

17 October 1941

Kashin is unrecognizable; there are so many people on the streets, and motor vehicle traffic, including *EMKA* cars, moves in a continuous stream.

Yesterday we began to pack our things in kit-bags and suitcases. In the evening I went to the hospital. I said good-bye to my isolation ward, to my soldiers. I almost burst into tears. Zaslavskiy said: "If we survive, we shall never forget you." Dear friends, I wish you speedy recovery!

Zhmurko went away earlier. He left me such a nice, warm letter and poems. Where could he be now? He dropped into our school to say good-bye to Mom, but I didn't see him. Today I went to school in the morning to pick up Rena's personal file and mine. I walked through the town, dropped into some libraries....

Unimaginable chaos reigns at home; things are lying everywhere and everything is upside down. We shall soon be leaving.

23 October 1941

Today we heard over the radio that our troops had abandoned Taganrog. The enemy is quite near Rostov. The Donets Coal Fields have been by-passed; soon they will be encircled. There is fighting going on on the approaches to Moscow, in the Mozhaysk sector.... The German army staff had occupied the headquarters of the Kalinin Regional Party Committee. The city is in ruins. The situation is critical. The enemy is advancing toward our heartland, toward the capital. Is it possible that it, too, would have to be surrendered? My heart is so heavy....

Our town is flooded with refugees. School No. 3 is filled with them and is not functioning. In our school they have occupied the entire first floor, and we are attending classes in two shifts. Probably our school will be closed soon. Everything points to our imminent departure. And what then?

Mom calls us frivolous, since we are still interested in amusements. But, in fact, we need to enjoy ourselves at times to forget all the horrors of the war, if only for a minute. After all, we are young, we want to live, to live a good and happy life. And we so seldom have fun now that no one should be offended by our behaviour. Moreover, the little fun we are still having will end soon, too.

Dad will join a partisan unit. And what about me? If only people knew how I want to go away with him! How I want to do something useful! But I'll have to go with Mom, to saveguard our finery.... My God!

27 October 1941

Today we were told over the radio that Stalino [now Donetsk], the heart of Donets Coal Fields, had fallen. Almost the entire Ukraine had been occupied. Moscow is surrounded from three directions. Leningrad is encircled. The situation of our country is critical.

Well, how long will it be before the offensive begins? How long will it be before we start chasing the Nazis? There is no end in sight to this accursed war! All our boys are being called up for duty in a *destroyer* battalion.[2]

Yesterday was probably our last day off spent as a get-together. We gathered at Klavushka's place; we brought a gramophone, danced, and played games. Sasha and I found the magazine *Niva* [Cornfield] for 1904 and looked through it. There were Blok's poems in it, and Sasha read them to me aloud. He reads fairly well. We broke up at six.

28 October 1941

I arrived at school yesterday, entered the classroom, and found only girls there. The boys are no longer considered pupils of the school. Only eight people attended the first lesson; it was physics.

At home, we talked again about going away; Mom wanted to leave her job already today.

OUR FINAL DAY IN KASHIN

6 November 1941

Only about a week has passed since my last entry, and there is so much to report! First of all, during all this time we were busy preparing for our departure. Our things have already been forwarded by train. We are leaving today for Yaroslavl', and then we'll decide what to do next.

We had a farewell party yesterday. We gathered at first at Valya's place; we cooked something, and then I changed my clothes and went to Klavushka's house. There were many people. I danced with Misha Ushakov. Then I tried to keep away from him, as far as possible, since he began to act "abnormal." He called me and told me:

"Name the person you love!" Well, what a request!

By the time we were having tea, it was already 6:00 a.m. Then we had more fun.... I had to be home by 7:00 a.m., so I said good-bye and kissed everyone; both the guys and the girls. I felt so sad to have to part from them!

The town was waking up. Everything was wrapped up in a rosy haze. Smoke from chimneys went up slowly. Good-bye my dear town! We'll soon be on our way.

THE TRIP

12 November 1941

My Kashin days are over; I am now homeless. All the good things, all the happy events are receding into the past. Each covered kilometre separates me farther and farther from all that was best in my life....

We arrived in Yaroslavl' on the 8th, in the morning. The city made a good impression on me; it is big and beautiful, and I liked its architecture. We left Yaroslavl' the next evening. And although this is our fourth day of travel, we have covered only 160 kilometres since we departed from Yaroslavl'. Our train travels only at night. We occupy a large boxcar; there are only six women and the rest are male hospital workers. The conditions are bad, but could be worse; I am not complaining. Each night I dream about people in Kashin. And these dreams are so realistic that sometimes real life itself seems like a dream.

How fast and, at the same time, how slow my days do pass! On the one hand, it seems to me that it was only yesterday that I left Kashin, and on the other I am so fed up with our journey, we travel so slowly, and the end is not even in sight. The trip wouldn't be so bad if we were moving, but we appear to be standing still most of the time. Now they let a troop train pass, now some other train. We travel through very beautiful, hilly localities, with forests all around, covered by hoar-frost. Everything is so beautiful! Particularly the birch-trees, so tall and straight. Shrouded by a silvery hoar-frost, they look like brides dressed in white. An inexpressible poetic quality pervades these white woods, particularly in the evening, before the sunset, when the air is saturated with a kind of special, drifting sadness and freshness. It feels so good....

Now we are standing at the station in Vereshchagin, only 120 kilometres from Perm'. Reportedly, the Kirov Theatre of Leningrad is now located there. If only we could stay in Perm'!

11 December 1941

...The Germans are on the run. Hurrah! Our troops have begun to press the enemy, advancing slowly but surely. Finally, it is happening. How quickly you cheer up when you learn that things are being set right. The sooner [we go home], the better. Rumours are circulating that we'll soon go home. If only they were true! It would be sheer happiness...to return to Kashin, to Daddy. If only the Germans were defeated soon.[3]

14 December 1941

Today is a day off.

I am now much happier in my class; I've adjusted. I don't even know all the surnames as yet; however, it seems that some of the girls and boys are quite nice.... What really matters is that our troops went over to the offensive along almost the entire front. They are pressing the Germans. Every day it is reported over the radio that our troops had occupied this or that town or a number of settlements.

The Nazis were beaten so thoroughly near my dear Moscow that it has now become abundantly clear to everyone that they will never enter it. Thousands, literally thousands of them will die on the approaches to our beloved capital. Soon our entire territory will be liberated. And then it would be possible for us to return home. What a happy day it would be!

17 December 1941

We heard the good news over the radio again today. The Germans suffered a significant defeat and are on the run. Well, that's splendid! Soon we'll likely hear a communiqué to the effect that our troops have entered Berlin. What a holiday it would be! I can't wait!

18 December 1941

On the 16th our troops captured Kalinin. No need to comment further. Wonderful!

29 December 1941

The New Year is only two days away. Only two days! If we were at home, we would likely be having a good time! But here.... I don't even know where I'll greet the New Year. It is possible that we'll go home soon.

On the 3rd of this month we were issued paramilitary attire, we were supposed to play volleyball, but since the day off was transferred to the 1st, the game didn't take place.

31 December 1041

This is the last day of 1941. I'll try to make a short summation. First of all, Grade 9; my friendship with Fedya, Max, Lena...; May Day parties, spring.... In the first part of the year, allotment garden, music, dancing, quarrels, making-up. Then the second part, after 22 June: shattered hopes, the first-aid course, the voluntary aid detachment and the hospital. I got tired, was in a terrible mood, and feared for the future.... School... the wood-sawing. The farewell party.... And the third part: our journey in a boxcar lacking basic amenities. Finally, Perm': new quarters, new school, new class, new friends. The begining of our offensive. My mood improves. And already...we are approaching the New Year.

Thus passed 1941, the most tempestuous year of my life. But the war is bound to end someday, and then everything will return to normal. Well, that's enough for now; till the New Year!

5 January 1942

Today (hurrah!) we received a telegram from Daddy. It was the first news we had from Kashin. At long last!

9 January 1942

Yesterday a letter came from Daddy. It was such a joyful event! And he wrote that...yes, he wrote about everything in Kashin. Only he didn't mention Busik [the family kitten].

INA'S LETTER TO HER FATHER

Undated

My darling Daddy!

I was sitting at home, cramming German...and suddenly the postman came and brought me a letter. From you! Without putting on any outdoor clothes, I dashed to tell Mom. She is now working around the clock in the hospital; yesterday the wounded began to arrive, so she was summoned. But she has already managed...to reply to you, and told me to add a postscript. She is standing beside me, reading your letter.

Reginka has run off to the skating rink; she will soon be back and we'll then dash off to school. Both of us are doing fine in school. Yesterday I made up for my arrears in chemistry; I passed an exam. Now I only need to review German and Russian literature, and I hope to do well in both.

We live well; don't worry about us. I'll look for uncle Vasya right away. His plant is located somewhere in the outskirts; we are bound to find him. How is Busik? Why didn't you mention him? Lots of love and many kisses to you.

Your Ina.

24 January 1942

Lo and behold, another calamity hangs over us. I have become acclimatized, accustomed to Perm', even developed a liking for certain things here and...we are about to move away. I had a sore throat, and I didn't go to school for three days. Suddenly, Mom comes, very agitated about something. And with good reason. It turned out that a man was sent from Kashin to brings us back with a travel warrant and, to make it short, we are told we are needed at home. For a long time Mom and I couldn't make up our minds what to do; we had almost decided to stay here, but...all the same, we are going home. Yesterday I cried almost the entire day....

30 January 1942

Again, we are travelling. We did leave after all. And right away all the joys [of Perm'] seemed diminished. I retained a fond memory of Vovka and Gal'ya; I am bound to forget the rest soon.

* * *

Kashin, 4 February 1942

I don't know how to begin. My God! What have I done? What have I done to deserve such a misfortune? I am speechless; Mishka is dead. My own, my darling.... He died of wounds. And I'll never, never see him again. Never! This is the end, the end.... No, I can't stand it.

9 February 1942

Now that I have become accustomed to my loss a bit, I can write about it. The pain is just as bad, but has somehow retreated deep into my heart. We returned home on 4 February at 6:00 p.m. Daddy met us at the station. I was so happy to be back at last, looking forward to a reunion with my loved ones. And instead.... I'll never forget having an almost physical sensation of a terrible chill inside me when Daddy said:

"Misha Ushakov...is no more. He died of his wounds...."

At first this hadn't registered in my mind. Then I cried. But how can tears ever fully express all the pain of a bereavement? I went to see Praskov'ya Vasil'yevna [Misha's mother — Russian Ed.]. I'll never forget that night. I stepped over the threshold and threw myself on her neck, crying. We were both crying and talked only about him. Only about him! The whole night....

I kept reminiscing about everything that touched him. I remember the entire story of our love, beginning with an April evening and ending with our last party.... He had such a capacity for love. How he loved! I remember when he said: "I love you. What do you wish me to do for you? Speak up and I'll make every wish come true for you, whether possible or impossible!"

And he will never say it again. I remember our evenings together; we were so happy that we kept silent, kept silent for hours, listening to the wonderful music inside us. He said once: "Too bad I don't know how to cry; I am so happy I could cry."

What glorious, unforgettable moments we had! On one date, he told me his secret which no one knows except me. And I...I too loved him. My love was strange and wild, but it was love all the same. I suffered myself and made him cruelly suffer. Many times I annoyed him needlessly; and many times I badly upset him. After all, as it turned out, he did cry at our last party.... He cried, though he never before knew tears. He then promised to send me his poems which he had written especially for me, and...he didn't send them. Perhaps he had mailed them, but they failed to reach me.

He left me only two photographs, one of which was inscribed: "To my darling"; a key, a flower made of bronze, and a lock of hair, black and soft. His hair. That's all. And I'll never, never see him again, never kiss him, never feel his hands, so strong and yet so loving.... This is the end of everything. Of one thing I am certain: nobody will ever love me the way he did. Nobody! Ours was a special kind of love. And how well he could express himself. My God, what a misfortune!

And why it had to be him to die! So brave, strong, clever, and refined. Such a remarkable human being. One in a thousand; and he perished.... He died at 11:50 p.m. on 31 December. He missed the New Year by 10 minutes. And I had some kind of a premonition then; there, at the school party, deep inside me I felt terribly sad.

Misha is no more; my Mishka! No more and never will be. Is it possible?

INA'S APPLICATION TO THE DISTRICT RECRUITMENT OFFICE

"...I have a great favour to ask of you, and I hope you'll grant my request. I wish to be inducted into the field forces. Give me any kind of a task, assign me any kind of a mission, and I will do my utmost to prove worthy of trust.

"I'll soon be eighteen; I have graduated from a first-aid course, and worked in a hospital for three months. Also, I am able to fire weapons fairly accurately.

"Surely, I am bound to make myself useful at the front! I am even willing to settle for a field hospital duty. Or send me to a partisan detachment. I am prepared to go anywhere, as long as I am needed and as long I am given the opportunity to fight the Germans."

15 February 1942

I'll never forget him. Never! I try to take my mind of him and think of something else, and I can't.

He is always in my thoughts. Always! And I am incapable of forgetting, of taking my mind of him. During the past few days I cried much less; I again started joking and laughing, but he still lives deep in my heart and, regardless of what I am saying and how much I am laughing, he and his love are with me.

Yesterday Klara and I called on Praskov'ya Vasil'yevna, but she was not at home, so we went for a walk. And when we were passing a movie theatre, we heard music and dropped inside. We met Zhenya Diligentov there. He was with Mishka when he was wounded, and Rem helped him to remove Misha from the battlefield. He was the last from our group to have seen Mikhail. It was so good to talk to him. I now know almost all the details. But...I am ready to hear the story over and over again. Zhenya promised to repeat everything once more, from the beginning to end. How painful and, at the same time, how good it is to hear people talk about Mishka. Klara and I speak of nothing else.

My dear, beloved Mishka! No one will ever match your love. Such a love is as rare on earth as a comet is in the sky. And it happens but once. Anyway, I was too happy, and I took my happiness for granted.... No, I ought not to keep thinking about him. It is too painful. Eh, Mishka, Mishka, my own, my darling!

16 February 1942

Today is already the 16th. How time flies! Already twelve days — almost two weeks — have passed since I learned of his death, during which I have had not a single moment of joy.

Yesterday I spent the night with Praskov'ya Vasil'yevna. I slept in the same place he slept, handled things which his hands had touched.... And today I saw him in a dream.... I kissed him countless times, was insanely happy that he was alive, looked into his eyes, black and so loving, and kept asking him: "Misha, my darling, is it only a dream?" And I still hear the sound of his reply in my heart: "A dream...." From now on, everything that concerns him would be but a dream. I swore to dedicate my good deeds to his memory. And if I ever have a son I'll name him Mikhail.

How I miss my Mishka! And I always have a feeling that he might emerge from behind a corner and start to laugh, and then we would walk together. I am merely day-dreaming, and in reality there is but a grave and marker with an inscription.... Misha! Mishka! I love you so, and I am calling you.... And you can't hear me. And you can't answer me, and you can't come.

18 February 1942

Sleep in peace, my dear boy! And why, when we were together, I took our relationship for granted? I was ashamed of it, as it were. How silly of me! And in my diary I mentioned our love so seldom and wrote so little about it. To make up for it, now...I am going over all the moments, all the petty details of our love, and I see that it was so wonderful....

No news from "there" as yet. How anxious I am to receive a positive reply! How I long to be "there," where life is so full, where there is danger and an opportunity to distinguish myself, and wreak vengeance on the Germans for ruining my happiness. Is it possible they won't take me? I am so anxious, so impatient! I can't continue living as I lived before; and to change my life here is beyond my capabilities. Besides, how could I do it? If only they would take me. After all, I am bound to make myself useful!

24 February 1942

Today I missed the first lesson. Oh, how undisciplined I've become! And I am like this in spite of the knowledge that later on I am bound to look back on this time of my life with tears in my eyes, but now...I am fed up with everything. And I haven't yet received reply from "there." Is it possible that they won't take me?

I am planning to visit Praskov'ya Vasil'yevna tonight, meaning that I'll spend another evening with Misha, in a way; with the memory of him. It will be good...and sad....

Well, now my well-travelled exercise book is almost finished. I've shared a lot with it. This is the last line. I've reached the end.

20 March 1942

I don't know. I don't know what I want for myself, what I yearn for. That is, I know, of course, but.... Well, I don't know how to say it. (What nonsense!) No, if only it were possible to write down everything, to bare the entire soul, to reveal all my wishes and thoughts: everything. Unfortunately, I can't do it. Well, all right; I'll try to write down something, as best as I can.

Behold, spring is coming. Spring! And what a spring at that! My eighteenth spring. For sure, this ought to be the best spring of my life. And the very idea that it is approaching excites me! I don't know what this excitement means; I don't understand it. Only I feel the approach of sadness, of longing, of limitless joy. And what will this spring bring to me? If only one could lift, for a moment, the magic curtain of time....

I believe that there is something good, something bright in store for me.

I would like to experience adult life soon, to know what my life holds in store for me, to live it through, to enjoy myself!

> Spring is everywhere, untamed and unlimited
> Like my vision of the future.
> I am getting to know you, life; I accept you.

Oh, how good it feels to be alive!
Oh, how I miss, miss Mikhail! How joyful he would be now, if he were

alive.... To be alive and to live.... Can there be anything more splendid, more wonderful? Life is everything.

The front has been stabilized. Is it possible that in the spring our troops will retreat again?

And what have I got around me now? I don't like school. It's dirty, crowded, cold, and lonely there. Even though my marks are fairly good. So I am waiting, waiting for something...good to happen.

22 March 1942

Today is Sunday; I am sitting at home.

Yesterday I received two letters: one from Galya and another one from Maya. Galka writes that nothing has changed and they are not planning to go home. Only apparently their life is merrier.... And Mayka's letter made me very happy. I got to like her still in Perm', particularly her appearance. I've never seen such marvellous hair. And she has a wonderful personality.

I am about to go to the library. Lately, I've been reading a lot, as in the past. "I want to live and live, to speed through life!" No, I don't. Such is the mood I am in today, but I don't wish to talk about it now.

Mishka! There he is, his face in front of me. I see his dishevelled hair, his eyes, so dark and warm, and his mouth, slightly mocking, so like and unlike himself when he was alive. It might seem ridiculous, but for me this portrait has a life of its own. Sometimes he looks at me with an air of blame and reproach, and then I feel ashamed and pained; and sometimes he gives me a barely perceptible, friendly smile, and then I have a sensation of warmth and sadness. And no matter what my thoughts might be, when I look at him I always wonder how he would react to them. And I wish for a miracle so....

Today is the first real spring day. It feels good.... And sad.

27 March 1942

Today I feel especially out of sorts. And it all started like this. Yesterday, no, the day before yesterday, we skipped some classes. We were very foolish. It turned out that, coincidentally, a commission visited the school, which was set up to investigate the poor attendance of the senior grades. A representative came to our classroom, and there were only six people. What a ridiculous situation! Well, of course, an alarm was sounded and a meeting was called for today. It came to almost nothing, and I don't want to dwell on it. However, at the meeting Mariya Nikolayevna Mitropol'skaya (who became our principal after Yakov Platonovich and Vetlitskiy had been drafted), said to us:

"Tell me, what is it that motivates you?"

Really, what does motivate us? Myself and the rest. And I pondered over the question. Well, let's start with all of us, meaning our group, and particularly our class. Now, in our times, in times of war! And what do we see: our girls (I am not even speaking of the boys, so few of them remain) are interested solely in dancing (these nasty, mean parties) and in movies, amusements that are pitifully ridiculous and absurd.

At least some get decent marks. But others.... Now, when people die, when death stalks its prey everywhere and heroism abounds, when everyone ought to concern himself with our country's plight, some find complete contentment in pursuing such activities as dancing the foxtrot with Serezha on Thursday, and being taken home by this or that boyfriend.

This is really criminal! This is terrible!

And what about me? Yes, I am ashamed to admit it, but...I don't lead an exemplary life, either. Admittedly, I've a goal ahead of me, a shiny and wonderful goal, but that's my entire commitment. Well, all the same I ought to do something in the meantime, too. One mustn't be passive.

Admittedly, I don't derive any pleasure from foxtrots and flirting, but after all books alone cannot substitute for real life. My current existence is pitiful. Indeed, even Mikhail himself had suffered terribly from inaction. Well, what am I to do? Wait until this summer? There is no choice but to wait. And in the summer...my dream will come true.

6 April 1942

Today is the 6th! A year has passed, exactly a year from the day on which our friendship with Mikhail began. I remember that day last year very, very clearly: an evening movie; fir branches, Aralov, radio-gramophone, Nekrasov (bass); Misha's sullen looks; a bench near the stairway; and his eyes, such stubborn, determined, dear eyes! Mishen'ka, my own, my darling, the best!

What has become of all this? Where is he?

Here is his portrait, in a simple brown frame. His face. His eyes. Where is he? He is no more and never will be.

Mishen'ka, Mishka, Mikhail!

I ought to, I am obliged to do something to honour your memory — something great, bold, and glorious!

Now, how to find words to convey all my longing, all my pain! I am laughing, talking, joking, but in my heart....

Only you, you alone truly live in my heart! And you'll never die. Ne-ver! I mustn't forget anything. I mustn't forget a single word, a single kiss. Mishen'ka! If you were alive today, you would have also reminisced about 6 April of last year.

And I am thinking....

No, I won't say it.

Mishka, my darling!

8 April 1942

What luck; I am so glad, glad; I've never felt so good! Today I had been accepted for work behind enemy lines. Oh, I am so happy! I'll write about everything, everything, later on. I am so glad!

Now, then I'll continue. Today, at the end of the school day, Mariya Nikolayevna walked into our class and said that Bochkov, deputy secretary of the District Party Committee, wants to interview five people from our class: Klara, Sasha, Valya Kulikova, Galya Kumkina, and Lelya Glazentsova. What for? Why? Nobody knew. I accompanied them. We waited and waited.... And it turned out that they were being called up for work behind German lines. The very thing about which I dreamed for so long, and with such a passion. And I was not among those chosen. But I went with them anyway.

Sasha's name was called out first, and then Klara's. They came out so radiant! After that I went in: Bochkov explained to me what was involved. I immediately replied that, of course, I would be willing to serve. We were so overjoyed, the three of us!

We are going! Going "there"! To the front. Everything is bound to turn out well. I feel good again and am happy, but in a different, more appropriate way.

Today is a wonderful, sunny, genuine spring day. Truly, a spring day.

20 April 1942

Without fail, you recognize happiness only after it has gone.

3 May 1942

It is now 5:30 a.m., a wonderful, fresh, rosy morning. Everything is so beautiful, so wonderful!

Well, let's start at the beginning. Yesterday a party was held for the senior grades of our school, and afterwards we decided to meet at Ara's place: well, to have a small party. At first I was in an awful mood. We went to Ara's house at midnight; we danced for a while and listened to gramophone records.

We had such a good time that no words can describe all my happiness, all my joy, limitless and colourful, like the bright, golden dawn which shone before us. Can there be anything better than our youth, our spring, our morning? No! During youth's happy moments, you love the entire world, and you want to dissolve in everything: the awakening nature, the stream, and the morning mist, so as to feel you are partaking of all of them.

7 May 1942

Another death notice came yesterday: Vanya Nesolepov had been killed. Another one.... So many die.

And the weather was awful today: a terrible wind blew up from nowhere and it began to snow! Then the sun reappeared. I, too, am affected, experiencing similarly contrasting mood changes. Oh, what is in store for me?

31 May 1942

Well, I managed to finish high school. I have left behind me the class, teachers, kids, lessons — everything....

I have graduated from high school, so what should I do next?

I am at a crossroads. I do have a goal, but it won't be easy to reach. Never mind... don't give up. You'll succeed.

NOTES

1.   The Russian word otverzhennyye means "outcasts."

2.   *Destroyer* battalions were irregular units organized by Party officials and composed mainly of Komsomol members. Their aim was to protect important installations, engage groups of enemy paratroopers, apprehend spies and saboteurs, and later on to destroy all life support behind enemy lines. See Edgar M. Howell, *The Soviet Partisan Movement, 1941-1944* (Washington: Department of the Army, 1956), pp. 44-45; D. Karov, *Partizanskoye dvizheniye v SSSR* [The Partisan Movement in the USSR] (Munich: Institute for the Study of History and Culture of the USSR, 1954), pp. 15-17.

3.   I have inserted Ina's undated letter (which follows this entry in the original and is addressed to her father) after her entry of 9 January 1942, since it is here that it fits the context.

(Partisan: 1942)

Undated

My dear family!

Please forgive me! I know it was mean on my part to treat you as I did, but it's better this way: under no circumstances could I've withstood Mom's tears. Don't be too upset, don't feel sorry for me, because my fondest, long standing wish has come true. I am happy! Remember this. Tomorrow, I'll give you all, all the details as to what is happening to me, and meanwhile I can only tell you that I am going to join a detachment. Daddy, please forgive me in the name of everything that is holy, forgive me for "deceiving you," as you put it. I came to the Regional Committee...and it was too late to back out.... My dearest family, only don't you cry and feel sorry for me. After all, this is how I wish to live my life. This is how I visualize my happiness.... It would be so good to see you, and to kiss you affectionately on my return in the fall.

Mom! Please don't cry, my dear. What's the point? Don't you want me to be happy? I feel good, believe me.

That's all for now. Tomorrow I'll write about everything, in minute detail. Don't be angry! Don't feel sorry for me!

Lots of love to you all.

Your disobedient Inka.

Undated

Hello, my dear ones!

So by now you must have reconciled yourselves a bit to the idea of my "running away." Well, that's good. I sent you a letter yesterday; in the evening I telephoned you, and today I tried to reach you again, but couldn't. Tomorrow I'll ring you up at 8:00 a.m.

That's how it all happened. I went with the girls; I didn't wish to leave them in Safon'yev, so I decided to accompany them to Kalinin. We arrived there and went to the dispatch station. I was given something to eat and slept well. The next morning, I went to the Party Regional Committee, to find out about our detachment; I needed a travel warrant. They asked me: "What do you need it for?" And I said: "I wish to catch up with the detachment." Well, somehow everything fell in its place after that. It was suggested to me that I travel the next day and already I was assigned a task.

Only don't be angry. What's the point of getting upset now? Today I again slept at the dispatch station. Our girls, excepting Yulya Peshcherikova, were sent to their unit. Therefore, Yulya and I were the only people left behind. She will go home today or tomorrow. Well, that's all the news about me.

And what about you? Anything new? How is the garden doing? Did I get any mail? Did Rena come? Did Mom obtain my matriculation certificate? What's new in school?

Above all, write me simply about everything, and I'll write you about everything, too, every day, with all the minute details.

I feel great. All I need to be completely happy is to know that you've calmed down. Please, for God's sake, don't get upset, especially Mom.

Kalinin is in ruins; not a single building remains intact. The last bombing of the city took place the day before our arrival.... I am now writing to you from the dispatch station. The chief of staff put us up in his room; we are spending the night here.

Remember me to all our acquaintances. Write to me soon.

Your Inka.

ENTRIES IN INA'S DIARY

6 June 1942
It was raining, and in the truck, under the wet tarpaulin, it was cold, damp, and crowded. Yet...I felt fine. In the morning we reached Goritse and waited there until 7:00 p.m.; then we continued the journey. And so today, in the evening, we arrived in Kalinin. The city is in ruins; hardly any buildings remain undamaged. How awful! We must repay the Germans for this. For everything!

Now we are staying at the dispatch station, in the officers' room, and are getting ready to go to bed. For some reason, we feel good.

7 June 1942
Well, such is life.... No, [that's] not how [I ought to begin].... One thing is certain: I am now a partisan. I am going to leave tomorrow. What else do I need? I am satisfied. However, I can't write now. I'll do it later!

INA'S LETTERS TO HER FAMILY

8 June 1942

Hello, my dear ones!

I am sitting beside a telephone, waiting for your call to come through, and I am writing to you. I am scheduled to leave Kalinin today, and therefore I would feel most disappointed if we couldn't talk before I left. Probably Yulya already delivered my letter to you, the one in which I had told you about everything. I have to go out soon, to attend to a certain business, and after dinner I'll pick up my things at the dispatch station, in order to be completely ready. Khrustalev [an instructor of the Regional Party Committee] and I will travel by truck. I've been issued rations for the trip.

Well, and what's new with you? Do write as often as you can, my darlings. Your I.

My darling Renok!

In a few hours I'll be going away to the assigned area. You'll be staying behind in our Soviet land, with your family. Remember, Renochka: we are going to fight for a good and peaceful life for all of us. You and I have often disturbed others' peace by our silly and needless caprices and disobedience. In this letter I would like to tell you something, to give you some advice, since you are my younger, beloved little sister: behave yourself properly. Don't be capricious, don't upset Mom and Dad — after all, you are their only child now. It would be easier for me to carry out any task, however difficult, if I were assured that there is peace and harmony at home. Remember this, my dear little girl, and be smart.

Kiss Mom and Dad for me, and remember me to all my friends, whenever you happen to run into them.

Lots of love and kisses to you, my nice little sister.

Remember me always; remember my advice.

Your Ina.

ENTRIES IN INA'S DIARY

8 June 1942

However, I didn't leave. Apparently, I'll leave tomorrow. I spent the entire day bustling about. I am so tired!

9 June 1942

Oh, there is so much that's new, so much that's perfect in my current life. Great! Well, one thing at a time. Yesterday I was sitting in the cafeteria of the Regional Committee, finishing ice cream, when suddenly a man enters the room and asks me:

"Is Konstantinova here?"

"Yes. I am here. What has happened?"

"You are wanted in the Regional Committee right away." I immediately got up and hurried there.

It turned out that we must go on the 9th at 6:00 a.m. We stayed overnight in the hostel of the Regional Committee. I shared a room with a nice girl, a partisan, who had already worked for nine months behind German lines in a partisan detachment.

I woke up at 5:00 a.m. Finally, we departed. When we were driving on Leningrad Highway by the dispatch station, suddenly an officer passed us. I was so glad to meet him again! I must digress here. Fate keeps placing wonderful people in my path! I simply am lucky.

This officer was an intelligent, considerate, and refined individual. He understood me and treated me so well that I was simply charmed by him. When I came to get my things on the day of my departure (I thought we were leaving on the 8th), we said good-bye to one another. He kissed me like an older person — a father or a friend — on a temple; it was a gesture which I'll never forget. His counsel would be like a law to me, without fail. And so I was very glad to see him again. We waved to one another, and...he was gone. No, I mustn't [cry]!

There were four of us in the truck: Khrustalev (instructor of the Regional Party Committee); commander of our united partisan group; its commissar;[1] and myself. Both partisans were fine, ordinary, wonderful lads. The commander had been awarded the Order of the Red Banner for his participation in the Finnish War.[2]

We passed through Torzhok; this nice little town was so devastated! It was completely reduced to ruins. Later on, we passed through many, many settlements with the majority of their buildings demolished.

We stopped in Kuvshinovo.[3] Here Khrustalev had to report to the Front [Army Group] Headquarters and we accompanied him. And so — I don't remember the details — I met (along with my companions, of course) the Brigade Commissar Abramov. He, too, was astonishingly interesting. So well-educated and also...refined. (Subsequently, I had the opportunity to get to know him well.)

He asked me about the very things everyone is now talking about: "Why am I joining the detachment; what for; do I know what to expect there; shouldn't I better turn back?" I replied using the very same arguments I had repeated mentally many times.

And so I am now writing in his room. They [*sic*] and the detachment commissar went away, and I stayed behind. I am writing and he is thinking about something. I wanted to tell you about so many things, but the result was nonsensical.

INA'S LETTER HOME

Undated [11 June 1942]

Hello, my darling Mom and Dad!

Yesterday we left Kalinin and spent the night at a place from which I am writing to you now. We are having a wonderful trip. Admittedly, the weather is cool, but I've warm clothing at my disposal. Do you know that my superiors have even told Colonel-General Konev [the Army Group commander] about me, and I'll soon go to meet him, because he wished to see me? I am flattered; shouldn't I be?

Our partisan commanders want me to stay at their HQ; I would be completely safe there, but I don't want that. Well, all right, we'll see what happens when we get there, and in the meantime I am so well taken care of! The commander gave me a personal weapon — a pistol with two clips[4] — and in Toropets I am to receive a submachine gun (a German one), which I've already learned to use. On the whole, during these past few days I learned so many new things, so many interesting things, that I'll never forget this time of my life.

We passed through places destroyed and scarred by the Germans. Oh, what horrors I have seen! So much destruction, so many tragedies they have caused; we must repay them for all this! My darlings, if you had seen all that I did, you too would have come with me to join the detachment..

Such interesting work awaits me there! Oh, I am so happy! In Toropets I am to receive a complete uniform, so that it is not necessary to send me anything.... I'll get everything I need.

Well, what's new with you? Did Renok come back? How do you feel? How is Mom? Write me as soon as you can. I am very, very anxious to receive some news from you.

Ina.

ENTRIES IN INA'S DIARY

12 June 1942

We are temporarily staying in Ostashkov. In Kuvshinovo five more people joined us in the truck; one interpreter, one radio operator, and three scouts who will work in our brigade.[5]

So, important tasks are apparently awaiting us.

Great! All five are remarkable people. I've already established a close rapport with them. Most likely I'll stay in the Brigade's HQ; so it seems. We arrived here yesterday, early in the evening. We went to the movies, wandered through the town, and then went to bed.

I am beginning to be homesick at times in the evening. I wrote a letter home yesterday.

14 June 1942

We are scheduled to leave today or tomorrow.

INA'S LETTER HOME

Undated [16 June 1942]

Hello, my darlings!

I am writing this letter to you from the village of Kunya,[6] where we arrived yesterday evening; this is the last day of my stay in Soviet-held land until I return after our victory. Tomorrow we'll cross over "there." Don't worry, I'll be completely safe.

We caught up with our Kashin detachment today; we were so happy to meet them! Sashok [apparently, Ina's former schoolmate] is much thinner, taller, and sunburnt.

I feel great. Never did life seem to me as interesting and for real.

In the detachment, I'll work in the reconnaissance group and stay at the HQ. Admittedly, my work won't be easy, but will be extremely interesting and useful. I trust my immediate comrades-in-arms implicitly. I know they will never betray me. I get along very well with the officers and men at the HQ.

All in all, I am very satisfied with my current situation and all the aspects of my current life. I have found my niche; here I am among friends.

I am at peace with myself, and I'll definitely return victorious, but believe me I'll die honourably, if necessary. This is how we all feel. Already many hardships have to be endured, but you should see me, running about carrying out assignments; I have been detailed as the duty person, and I cook dinner, so you wouldn't recognize me. I sleep very little; I am dark from sunburn, my face is weather-beaten and perhaps coarsened a bit, but it doesn't matter. Besides, I eat very well. So I am not likely to lose any weight. In short, "life is beautiful and wonderful!"

Today the Germans carried out as many as four air raids against our village. The bombing was awful, and their machine guns gave us a good thrashing. The bombs exploded about 70 metres from us, and bullets whistled literally above our heads (I lay in a ditch). But you see, I survived. Consequently, nothing will ever happen to me; I believe this whole-heartedly. From now on, for some time I won't be able to write to you directly, but don't worry; you'll be informed about me by a man who will keep in touch with you.

Tell Renochka on my behalf to remember me, to write to me very frequently, and to obey you, before it is too late and before she has any regrets. We are about to go into battle, to fight for our happiness, happiness which one ought not to spoil by being capricious over petty things. I am now very sorry about having been so silly, so disobedient, and so capricious in the past.

Dear Mom, please write to Vera Aleksandrovna that I am very sorry, that I love and respect her very much.

Good-bye, my darlings. Don't worry about me and feel sorry for me.

Lots of love and kisses and hugs to you. Keep well. Here is one more kiss. How I wish I could kiss you in person!

Your happy Ina.

ENTRIES IN INA'S DIARY

16 June 1942

I now have the urge to write down here everything, truly everything; the happenings of every hour of the past few days. How time flies! One thing replaces another; everything changes in an instant, like in a kaleidoscope. Well, one thing at a time.

We left Ostashkov on the 12th. We spent the night in a village and arrived in Toropets the next day. Toropets is a small town which has been badly devastated. The detachments to which we are assigned are in Kun'ya.

We managed to reach our destination late in the evening. All along the way, we had fun. During these past few days, I got to know Gen'ka, our radio operator. Our friendship is simple and nice. The next day Zoya, Gen'ka, and I went for a walk through the village and suddenly there was Sashok! How glad I was to run into him. We talked about all sorts of things. It was so pleasant! The next day, very early in the morning, their detachment went away, and in the early evening we went too, but in a different direction.

Nevertheless, there was plenty of hardships to endure, particularly for me, spoiled as I was by a nanny and accustomed to Mom's tender care. How many nights, cold and sleepless, I've already passed! There was plenty of hard work, dirt, and unpleasantness. However, all the hardships are obliterated and forgotten as you experience an intensive, warm sensation, which may be expressed thus: "I am a partisan." How wonderful!

17 June 1942

Yesterday I was so sleepy that I didn't finish writing. So we left Kun'ya and came here yesterday (I don't know the name of the place). The front was nearby. We stopped in a village and occupied a house. Half of the windows were intact. We moved the beds, swept the floor, and cleaned up the rooms. We used one room as a bedroom and another one as our HQ. My mood was spoiled somewhat in the early evening. Also, I am affected by the persistent, disgusting, grey, cold weather. This morning we got up very early; it was terribly cold and we decided to light a fire in the stove. Yesterday, when we were going to bed, Gen'ka forced me to take his coat, because I had nothing to cover myself with.

I like Gen'ka so much! Well, this morning I looked at him — he was completely frozen. I quickly covered him with his coat and began to light the stove. I then started making breakfast. After we had eaten, I went back to sleep. Later on the commissar woke me up and asked me to copy his plans. I am now about to go to the bath-house.

I am so happy here. I got used to all these people and feel at home among them, even better than at home, because there I was capricious and disobedient. Eh, how foolish I had been!

There are eight of us now at the HQ: apart from myself, the brigade commander, political section head Petr Lekomtsev, chief of staff Pavlik Kotlyarov, radio operator Gen'ka, a nice, ordinary lad, interpreter Vanya Mochalov, who also seems quite nice, and Zoya. Now I don't know what to think about her; I like her very much and yet there is something I don't like about her. However, on the whole, we do get on together; she is my kind, but Dusya is the "still water runs deep" type. And I've already got so used to all of them that it seems to me that I've known them for ages. Well, so that's it. In another three to four days, perhaps a bit later, we too will go into action. At last!

A difficult, onerous mission awaits us. We'll cover 100 kilometres on foot, behind German lines. I haven't been given exact instructions yet, but....

23 June 1942

I haven't written for a long time. So much has happened! I was not mistaken; this exercise book will see a great deal.

I particularly remember the events of 19 June. At night a large punitive detachment approached our village very, very close. The exchange of fire continued throughout the night. In the morning, when we woke up, villages burned all around us. Soon the first casualty was brought to me. My hands were covered with blood. Then I took this seriously wounded man to a doctor, 6 kilometres away. When I returned, we had to execute a certain village elder, a collaborator. We went to get him; we read him the sentence and led him to the place of execution. I felt awful.

In the evening, about eleven, just as I was getting ready to go to bed, another wounded man was brought in. Again I dressed his wounds, and again had to deliver him to a doctor. And the weather was terrible; it was cold, dark, raining, and windy! I dressed warm and we set off. My sick man instantly became frozen; I had to give him at first my raincape and then my jacket. I had only a blouse on, and was terribly chilled. On the way, the cart broke down and I fixed it, and then we got lost. In short, it took us four hours to get to our destination. I barely warmed up a bit when it was time to start back. I returned in the morning; I had quite a night!

And, on the whole, my life is so different now when compared to what it had been just a month ago. School, friends, Kashin, all have receded far into the past....

Yesterday Kotlyarov called me over for a discussion and seriously suggested that I become a scout. This would involve working all alone, away from the detachment, and having to contend with great many difficulties. And it would be more dangerous....

I agreed, and am getting ready. Today I am on duty, cooking breakfast and dinner. This is now all in a day's work.

Eh, if only I could see Mom, Dad, and Rena; even for a moment!

29 June 1942

I write seldom now, but there is a lot, a lot to write about. This is not surprising; after all, my life is now so completely transformed! Oh, I've no time to write!

INA'S LETTERS TO HER FAMILY

2 July 1942

Renok, my darling little sister!

In three days it will be your birthday. Congratulations, and all the very best to you! ...I often think about you all, and am so anxious to see you all, if only for a moment. I see your little mug very clearly in my mind's eye, and I've the urge to keep kissing it. And don't you forget me either. Write to me as often as you can. Write about everything; I want to know everything, absolutely everything that concerns you.

How is Mom? Please look after her. Remember that she is in poor health, and gets upset even more now, on my account. So you must keep calming her down; don't let her worry.

I live very well. Admittedly, often I am faced with hardships to which I am not at all accustomed, and then I regret very much that at home I had had such a carefree life.

You, Renok, ought to study. I am telling you this only because my experience has taught me the importance of education.

Well, that's all for now, my dear little girl. One more thing: do you ever see our friends? How are they? Remember me to them.

Well, do write soon to me. A thousand kisses to you from your Ina.

5 July 1942

Hello, my dear Mom, Dad, and Renok!

I sent you my last letter only yesterday, and here I am writing to you again. My life hasn't changed; I am to stay here for another five days. We'll definitely leave soon. The weather has become very, very warm —

even too hot, but that's good. The only problem is the multitude of mosquitoes; they are vicious. Both my arms and legs are covered with their bites. Our present location — hills and valleys with marshes in the low-lying areas — attracts them. I am afraid to come down with malaria, because should this happen they'll evacuate me to the rear. Fortunately, we are going to leave this area soon.

What is happening at home? I think about you all the time; now they are having breakfast, now Dad arrives home from work, and now they are going to bed; I very, very clearly see you all in my mind's eye. Well, never mind; it won't be long before we are reunited. The plans are: we'll go "there" and then we'll come back for a rest in about one and a half to two months. Before we know it, I'll be home on leave, visiting you. I've already made an arrangement to this effect with my commanders.

I've many friends here, and I am getting along very well with everyone. Soon Gen'ka, our radio operator, will come back; he went to the Front [Army Group] HQ and was going to send my telegram to you from there. You must have received it by now.

Today is Reginka's birthday. I've already sent her greetings in a separate letter, and in addition I am writing to her here.

My darling Renochka, I want to kiss your nice, little mug; my very, very affectionate kisses to you. I wish you health and happiness! Look after Mom and Dad and don't you upset them. After all, they get upset very easily.

When I come back, I'll bring you a nice gift; in the meantime I am writing to you, and in turn await a reply from you all.

Well, my dear ones, lots of love and kisses and hugs to you. Write to me. If I get some local mail, please forward it to me immediately or, better still, keep it until my return. Well, that's all.

Your Ina.

P.S. I was proud to swear the Oath of Allegiance today.

8 July 1942

Hello, my dear Dad, Mom, and Renok!

I write every time an opportunity presents itself to send a letter to you. This happens quite often, and therefore I am writing to you almost every day.

My life remains unchanged, that is, I feel remarkably well. Only don't get the idea that I am saying this just to reassure you. No, in fact, I am very satisfied with my current life.

From the very first day I became a partisan I forgot what it's like to be in a bad mood. The minute I appear crestfallen, our officers and girls begin to joke, laugh, and cheer me up; in no time I feel well again.

Actually, we have fun all the time. Especially in the evenings, when the entire HQ, the eight of us, gather at the home base. Everyone tells a story of some kind and makes jokes; we giggle and go to sleep very, very late. By and large, work and leisure leave us no time for moping. Besides, I now have to train a great deal, since the people with whom I'll be working have taken special courses. They are helping me to catch up with them, and the work awaiting me is very important and interesting. I'll learn a great deal here. And what matters most, I am getting a lot of valuable living experience. Consequently, in future I would not be daunted by any difficulties standing in my way.

Today is the first day of good weather here; it's warm and dry. For some reason, it has become very, very quiet. We are already so accustomed to the distant rumble of guns, to machine-gun bursts, and to aircraft engine roar, that we even miss them. Yesterday some leaflets were dropped from enemy aircraft, in which the events on Kerch' Peninsula were recounted. On the whole, these vile creatures treat us to such propaganda that you wonder whether they are idiots or just plain crazy. And here, so close to the enemy troops, they are hated much more [than in the rear].

Well, all right, that's enough about me. Why is there no news from you? Though it's still too soon to get a letter. But, should there be no letters from you on the first plane, I would be very upset.

Countless kisses to you, my dearest Mom and Dad.

Your Ina.

18 July 1942

Hello, my darlings!

Yesterday I received the first batch of letters. You can't imagine how happy I was! I almost hugged Dusya to death. And I was very saddened by the fact that not a single letter came from Kashin. Only a telegram arrived from Mom, which I kept kissing until it was full of holes. Too bad that I couldn't kiss Mom herself. I received four letters from Reginka. I am very, very glad that she keeps me in mind. Well, I hope she'll keep writing just as often in the future. [Evidently, Ina's sister was away from home.]

If you knew what it means to me to receive a letter from home, you would surely find at least a moment a day to write something to me! Among the eight letters received was one from Abramov, the Brigade's commissar, now at the Front HQ. It was such a remarkable, warm letter. But not a single one came from you or my girlfriends in Kashin. Why? Only Allah knows. And I am so anxious to find out what is happening in Kashin!

Here everything is as usual. I am very satisfied with my life. When we are "at home," that is, not on a mission, I've nothing to do. We don't even do kitchen duty now. We eat very well. We are supplied with milk, milk products, and meat in unlimited quantities. We consume a lot of berries, particularly wild strawberries. There is such a mass of them here that you can gather as many as you want, literally as soon as you step out through the door. We eat them with gusto, whether cooked or uncooked, with or without cream, or "roasted."

Yesterday Dusya and I, and two of our guys went to the Lovat' River, to pick berries; we sat down on the near shore and suddenly someone began to fire a submachine gun from that shore. There were police all around. Now we are forbidden to go to the river; we are allowed to bathe in the lake exclusively.[7]

In a few days we'll be carrying out a very serious operation. All those who are here are preparing for it now. I hope we would be successful!

Tomorrow our messengers will leave for Kalinin; they'll carry this letter. If it is possible for you to send a parcel to Kalinin, it will reach me quickly, but if you can't do it — don't worry. I can get everything I need here.

In the telegram Mom mentions my matriculation certificate. It's good that she received it, but there is no need to send it as yet; when I come back, I'll send it myself. Apparently, I wouldn't be able to attend the Institute this year. Well, it can't be helped. But the moment the war ends, we'll apply ourselves to our studies as conscientiously as we are now fighting the Nazis. There are many, many people here with high school education. After the war they'll all attend institutes.

Meanwhile, we are giving the Nazis a hard time. During the past month our brigade derailed eight important trains, blew up four railway bridges, and caused a great deal of damage to paved roads. It's not for nothing that the Germans consider the struggle with the partisans as a "second front," and have unleashed an all-out war against them.

Well, all right, that's enough about me! Well, what's new with you? How is Mom keeping? How is the food situation? I've such an urge to send you something again, if only some berries for Reginka, but that's not possible.

How are our teachers? I've written to Praskov'ya Vasil'yevna, even before my first trip. If you happen to run into her, tell her that I am waiting for her reply. I hope to see Sasha in a few days. Well, my dear ones, lots of love and kisses and hugs to you all. It's getting dark already; time to finish writing. Write to me often, about everything. Please remember me to our acquaintances.

Your Inka.

ENTRIES IN INA'S DIARY

21 July 1942

I've not written for almost a month. And so much has happened during that time!

On the 4th it was exactly a month since I left home. And on that day, 4 July, I went on my first mission. I started out in the evening. Zoya and Dusya had already gone, and I was the last to leave. I was expected to join a group from Lesnikov's detachment.[8] Before my departure I got acquainted with the section commander. Then Gen'ya and I had to cross the Lovat'. My group caught up with us, and we were taken across the river. So we were on our way.

There were seven of us, including Grisha Shevachov, a tall, thin boy, a Jewish type, quite smart and mentally developed, but not too strong physically. In short, a nice lad. Then there was Igor Glinskiy, a wonderful boy — astonishingly nice. Not handsome and with a commonplace appearance, at first glance he seemed rather uncouth. But there was something about him, I can't quite explain it, that I found so irrepressibly appealing. Perhaps it was his smile, partly hidden in his eyes. He has a striking sense of humour, and is clever and well-read. Next came Makasha Berezkin. Well, what a delightful person! He has a dark, dark complexion, like a gypsy, black, slightly curly hair, as well as blinding-white teeth, and his eyes are so alive and sparking. He is always in a good mood, always smiles. And he never refuses an assignment. Then came Lesha Subbotin; tall, well-built, and with an ordinary face. He was terribly anxious to carry out the mission well, and dreamed of capturing a submachine gun. Fate ordained otherwise.... Next was Borya Kulakov — very short, dark, sometimes very witty — a merry lad. And the last of them was Sergey Nekrasov, nicknamed "baby crocodile," with a peculiar face and personality. And then came I. Our task was as follows. The group was to mine the Pustoshka — Nevel' Highway between Ruda and L. Talankino. They carried some TNT and mines. As for me, on the 9th around noon I had to be at a safe house, in order to discuss with a certain individual the plan to blow up German barracks and to obtain identification papers. Later on, I was to rejoin the group.

Well, we were on our way. The first night passed very quickly. We covered about 18 km and stopped for the day's rest in a clump of hazelnut bushes near the village of Obrezy. At first it was raining; we huddled together and fell asleep. Then we had a wonderful day. As a result, I came to know the boys better. After dark, we continued on our way. We dropped into some villages to get guides, but made only modest progress that night. We stopped for the day's rest near the village of Slozino; here we sat under a fir-tree, in a shed, and we had a good time. And all over, along the road, violets grew. Many, many of them! It was wonderful! And all the time I was in a kind of elated mood. It was still daylight as we were leaving; we took a chance. When we reached the second railway line, we stopped.

Makasha went to find out about the road, and Igor, Lesha and I dropped into the village of Yurochkino, had something to eat there, drank some milk, took some in bottles for the boys, and rejoined them. We crossed the track and continued on our way, toward our next day's rest. We stopped in a forest, on the shore of a lake. Again we huddled together and went to sleep. Earlier, in the morning, I had gone down to bathe in the lake. Then, during the day, two boys from the village met us by accident; one of them was a remarkable lad, named Valentin. They gave us directions, and in the evening we were under way again. During this part of our expedition, something very unpleasant happened. I left a spade behind during one halt; we discovered this 3 kilometres later. Igor and I went to get it. Well, on our way, we got into an argument. We came back and Grisha asked: "Have you found it?" And Igor says: "We found the spade and lost our friendship." However, at the next day's rest Igor and I made up; we even became friends. What a wonderful lad this Igor is!

My last stretch with the boys began at the village of Vorob'yevo. I had to hurry to the rendez-vous at the secret address, and therefore decided to go ahead of them alone. They gave me a send-off. It was touching how they fussed over me, fed me, gave me some milk and bread to take with me, and helped me to pack my knapsack. What dear friends they were! Boris guided me to the road, and I went.

I walked, walked, and walked. I arrived on time, but the man didn't show up. The police became interested in me, and I was asked to enter a house. I suggested that they let me stay in the house for a rest. They let me spend the night there, appropriated my identification papers, and began to watch me. Since the boys' destination turned out to be a place surrounded by police, who were on the lookout for partisans, I had to warn them as soon as possible, and I decided to run away.

I asked to be allowed to bathe in the stream; I forded the stream fully dressed, up to my neck in water, and ran away. But the police had my identification papers.

I was in a hurry to reach the boys; I was counting on meeting them in the evening near the village of Indyka. When I arrived there, I waited and waited; there was no sign of them. And suddenly a woman told me that German soldiers were coming to the village. I became concerned for the boys and decided to look for them. In vain I searched and searched for them in the woods; then, running through a marshy terrain and through meadows, I returned to the village. They were not there. I seemed suspicious and was again arrested. Since I had no passport, it was decided to hold me until the arrival of the German troops. Then and there I became terrified. After all, the Germans didn't even bother to talk to people without identification papers. Their verdict in such cases was: a partisan! And then to the gallows with you. Well, what was I to do?

I was lucky that the Germans were scheduled to arrive only in the morning, about six.

I was given a bed in the elder's house; three men were staying there, the elder and two policemen. I came to the conclusion that I had nothing to lose: I would be killed either way, so I decided to slip away somehow. I pretended all night that I had an upset stomach; at first, they accompanied me to the outhouse and then they began to trust me. Finally, I ran away. Swift like the wind, I ran across the yard, the street, and a field of rye. So I got away.

I didn't even feel tired, but, dear God, how dejected and full of pessimism I was! It seemed to me there was no longer any happiness on earth, the boys were bound to perish, and I was incapable of carrying out any assignment. I walked fast, almost without rest, and already in the morning of 11 July I reached Lesnikov's HQ; I was the first to come back. I was given something to eat; then I lay down to rest, and in the evening went to Zadezha, to our base. I found only Gen'ka there. My legs were terribly sore, and I could hardly move.

The commander's voice awakened me during the night. He asked me to get up, questioned me, and invited me to sit down to a meal with him. In short, he received me warmly and with kindness. And immediately I cheered up.

The next day we went back to Kupuy[9] and life continued as usual. I was terribly worried about the boys. One day in the morning, about five, Makasha showed up. How I jumped up, when I learned of it! How happy I was! I almost hugged him to death. Now I burst into tears and now I was mindlessly happy. He told us that they had managed to mine the road, but met detachments of German soldiers on several occasions and, during the last encounter, exchanged fire with one such detachment near the village of Bayevo. They had to retreat; it was then that they lost each other and went back separately. And earlier still Lesha Subbotin was killed by his own grenade.

The next day arrived Igor and Grisha, and the following day came Boris and Serezha. How I rejoiced! I would now follow these dear guys anywhere, into both fire and water. How well they behaved on the march, in combat, and at the home base! Particularly, toward me. Now I visit my dear, true friends every day; we sit down to talk, and I am having the best time with them I ever had.

INA'S LETTER TO HER FATHER

Kupuy, 24 July 1942

My dear Daddy!

In only two to three days our entire brigade will go "there," on a new, big mission.[10] We'll spend one to one and a half months there, meaning that I would not be able to go home before the end of September or beginning of October. Am I not going to hear from you before then? In spite of my full and interesting life, I feel so sad sometimes; I want to see you so badly, especially since our Kashin detachment had been included in another brigade....

But our brigade is quite strong; we are well-armed, have plenty of ammunition, and the people, too, are all right. We received thanks for carrying out our last mission; ten people were recommended for decorations. And we'll prove deserving of trust in fulfilling this task as well.

I am very satisfied with my present life; only I am so anxious to receive some news from you!

Nevertheless, I am not losing hope. Several messengers from here have just set off for Kalinin. I hope they'll bring something. Love and kisses to you, my dear. Write to me, without fail.

Your loving Inka.

28 July 1942

My dear ones!

Well, so we are going away in a half hour. Everything, absolutely everything, has been gathered, checked, and readied. If you could only see me now — in full marching order! There are machine-gun ammunition belts around my waist and a carbine is slung over my shoulder. I am also carrying a kit-bag, cartridge pouches and grenades, and in my pockets I've a Walther and a field dressing. I am wearing a big, turtleneck wool sweater and a jacket; I find this outfit most comfortable. We are saying good-bye to our Kupuy, and to the dear places that we have become so accustomed to. We are saying good-bye to our native parts. We are about to go behind enemy lines for two months. And then to you, home. Don't expect any more mail from me, unless something happens to me; only then you'll get a letter or, more accurately, a message will be transmitted by radio to the Front HQ and the HQ, in turn, will communicate with you.

But this isn't likely to happen. I'll return soon, in one piece, alive and well.

The final rallying shots have been fired in the camp, and everyone is rushing and bustling about.

Good-bye! Greetings to all! Lots of love and kisses to you.

Your Inka.

ENTRIES IN INA'S DIARY

29 July 1942

We are going away today; we ought to have gone yesterday, but the rain delayed us. The entire brigade is going behind German lines for two months. Everything, absolutely everything has been gathered, checked, and readied. I received a Russian carbine, as well as 125 cartridges, and made myself another kit-bag, to replace the one I had lost. I feel well; I hope I'll survive!

30 July 1942

Today is a special day for me. I remember this day last year.... How everything has changed! I am writing from a place behind German lines, about 25 kilometres from Kupuy. We left about 6:00 p.m. yesterday. We marched all night; I was really tired. Now we are resting in a very pleasant grove.... I went to see the guys; we are stationed with Ryndin's detachment. It's 2:00 a.m. now. Almost everyone is asleep.[11]

* * *

[This was the last entry in Ina's diary. She turned eighteen that day — Russian Ed.]

INA'S LETTERS TO HER FAMILY

Undated

Hello, my darling Mom!

So I wrote to you all together, and now I decided to write you separately. If you only knew how I long to see you, to give you a very, very affectionate hug, and to smother you with kisses. Well, not to smother you; God forbid! Without a doubt you remember how I used to kiss you furiously. Smiling, you have always pretended to disapprove, while I was giggling. Wasn't like that? Tell me the truth. My darling, I very, very clearly see you, Dad, and Reginka in my mind's eye. Sometimes I suddenly wake up at night, because I am so, so convinced that you are sitting on my bed, as you used to do at home. And I feel so good and have such a pleasant sensation! But then I wake up, and there is no one, and it is empty all around. If you only knew how I love you and always loved you all.

My sunshine, don't be sad, you shouldn't! Do you know what is now most difficult for me to bear? The thought you might be crying while thinking of me. Don't! Don't!

I now live splendidly. I am liked here, for some reason. And the boys from the group with which I went on my first mission have become like a family to me. Well, write to me, write....

Here is my kiss.... Do you feel my affection?

Your Inka.

P.S.

I was a bit sick, had a tiny boil, but I am well again.

Undated

My dearest Mom!

I have something to add. I wrote to you when I was sick with tonsillitis. I couldn't send my letter right away. Well, here is my postscript. Do you know, Mom, how very touched I was by all the fuss made over me while I was sick, by seemingly total strangers. The brigade commander himself got up at night to boil some milk for me, brought me strawberries, handed his dry biscuit ration over to me, and obtained sugar for me somehow. Zoya lent me her coat, and turned her bed over to me, as she has a better one. Dusya didn't leave me even for a minute, and scolded me when I took the bandage off my throat, or tried to get up. Gen'ka fetched my breakfast, dinner, and supper; the boys from my group brought me books to read and visited me frequently. I was embarrassed to be the object of so much attention. And, at the same time, it felt very pleasant.

Lots of love and kisses to you, my dear Mom.

Your Ina.[12]

2 August 1942

Hello, my dear ones!

Today one of our three girls, Dusya, went on her first mission. Tomorrow Zoya and I will go as well. To carry out real, big, important, and difficult assignments.[13] I'll try to do my best. Oh, if you could see my current documents! My passport is so mutilated it looks as if someone had been chewing it. I've learned my story by heart, so everything is in order; the operation ought to succeed. Naturally, I am a bit nervous, but never mind. Everything is bound to turn out just fine.

I have no news to report.

I am waiting impatiently for letters from you. Upon my return from the mission, in about two weeks, I'll write to you immediately, at the first opportunity, to tell you what has been accomplished. And do think about me often and write to me a lot. Send your letters without postage stamps.

Should anything happen; well, if I become sick or take a long time to come back, don't worry. Our radio operator Gen'ka will keep in touch with us and will write to you about everything. Only don't get upset. I am very happy and feel great.

Well, do wish me all the best. Write to me!

Love to you all.

Your I.

Fig. 5. Left to right from the top: Petr Ryndin, detachment commander (from 13 August 1942 commander) of the 2nd Kalinin Partisan Brigade; Ina Konstantinova; and Ina's fellow partisans: Yul'ya Novoselova, Valya Karaseva, Vera Bocharova and Dusya Tsvetova.

Петр Рындин   Инна Константинова

Юля Новоселова   Валя Карасева

Вера Бочарова   Дуся Цветова

Fig. 6. Left to right from the top: Filipp Tyapin (from 13 August 1942 detachment commander of the 2nd Kalinin Partisan Brigade); and Ina's fellow partisans: Tanya Prokhorova, Varya Kaftyreva, Nina Salazko, Lida Blagoderova and Nikolay Dudushkin.

Филипп Тяпин

Таня Прохорова

Варя Кафтырева

Нина Салазко

Лида Благодерова

Николай Дудушкин

Undated

Hello, my darlings!

I don't know how to begin. Well, all right; first of all, I am alive and well, and feel wonderful. It is only three days since I returned from behind German lines. Again, I had a bit of an experience. Again, I was caught. This time I fell straight into German clutches. I didn't expect it would all end so well.... I've lived through so much.... Honestly, I thought I might go grey. I'll tell you everything when we meet. I am now detached from the Brigade, on our territory and among our people. I nearly went crazy with joy after I crossed the front lines and when I saw our people![14]

In a few days, I'll probably go back "there." However, don't worry about me. I am deeply convinced that nothing will happen to me, and I'll soon come home on leave. Probably, in a few days, I'll receive many, many letters from you. This would make me so happy!

I saw Khrustalev yesterday. He passed your greetings to me. Yesterday, too, I saw our boys from Kashin: Zhenya Diligentov, among others. They told me that Mom worries very much about me. This is totally unnecessary.

I feel remarkably well. After all, I am a hundred times happier than all the girls back home — dancing and supposedly having fun — since during these difficult times I too am useful to my country.... Even if I were to go hungry, fall into Nazi clutches, and walk barefooted hundreds of kilometres — still I would be very rich, as my present life is truly satisfying to me. Well, my dear ones, lots of love and kisses to you.

Your Ina.

24 August 1942

My darling Mom!

A few days ago, I received the first letter from you.

If you only knew how infinitely happy you made me! How I cried over it! As if the two and a half months during which I heard nothing from you didn't happen. Your letter was dated 6 August. Please don't get so upset, my darling. Yesterday I also received a letter from Daddy, dated 30 July. I am infinitely touched by your kind words....

Regarding the Institute, I have to forget about it this year. Well, never mind. After all, when I return for good I'll have access to any institute. I've not given up the idea of graduating from college even for a moment.

You tempt me with your garden. Indeed, I would like to taste your creations very, very much. But, alas, I can't! Nevertheless, I still hope to taste your tomatoes, since I'll definitely come home for a month. In the meantime, I am getting a rest here. Yet I abhor idleness. If only I could return "there" soon! To my friends, about whom I worry very, very much.

Do you know that I yesterday received a very nice, cordial letter from Vadim, the son of Zinaida A. Khorobrova? All of you there consider me almost a heroine. Why? I am just an ordinary Soviet person.

My dear Mom: first, in a few days I am going to take part in a new operation, and quite a difficult one at that, but I'll be accompanied by remarkable people; and, secondly, I am certain to have your blessings, and therefore nothing irrevocable is bound to happen to me.

Keep well and be happy. Live in harmony. Love and kisses to you, my darling Mom. My regards to acquaintances, teachers, and definitely Praskov'ya Vasil'yevna....

More love and kisses.

Your disobedient Inka.

Undated

My dear Daddy!

Yesterday I received your letter which you had written on 30 July while approaching Kalinin. I am now already in my tenth day of rest in our rear.... Should my next mission end successfully, of which everyone is certain, I hope to see you, my loved ones, in about a month.

A few days ago, someone came from the Kalinin Regional Committee and told me that he had seen you in Kalinin, and alleged that you, too, are going to join a detachment somewhere near Opochka. Is this true? This has upset me. After all, Mom is having such a difficult time. When I read in your letter that her health had deteriorated I felt as if I received a knife wound to my heart.

Daddy, you and Reginka should somehow keep her from worrying.

If only we could fully convince her that I'll return, and meanwhile am doing fine and am completely happy. And you, my dear Daddy, should believe in it, too. What really matters is that we'll soon see each other, without fail. I now receive lots of mail. I get letters from Grandmother, Aunt Tonya, friends — of whom, it seems, there are a great many — and especially frequently from Reginka. Each letter brings me infinite joy.

Well, my dear Daddy, I am waiting to hear from you regarding your future plans. Perhaps we shall meet here?

Write to me as soon as you can and wish me success in my new undertaking. Lots of love and kisses and hugs to you. Keep well, my dear Daddy.

Your Ina.

29 August 1942

Hello, my dear Renok!

For some reason, I haven't heard from you for a long time. Why? Are you beginning to forget me? This will not do!

Do you know where I am writing this letter from? Oh, good gracious! I can't believe my own "luck"; I was arrested. Yes, yes! Quite in earnest, and by our own border guards. It was both funny and sad. Such a silly predicament. You see, at first I travelled with Khrustalev, on his passport, because I no longer had mine. Well, later on I went for a drive, and at the same time to accompany a certain girl. We reached a frontier command post and I was arrested there; I was locked up in a bath-house until my identity was established. A sentry was posted outside. So I spent an entire night there. Then they let me out in the morning, and I am now sitting in the commandant's room, writing a letter for lack of anything else to do. When he returns from Toropets, they will let me go to rejoin the Brigade.

And meanwhile...what a comical situation! I was caught by our people.

In a few days I am going to take part in a new operation, a very important and interesting one, about which you'll probably hear. I'll be under the command of a decorated captain, Vasiliy Razumov. He is a remarkable person and a good friend of mine. On our return, I'll come home on leave.

Renochek, I've something to ask you: please find among my letters, the one in which I wrote down the address of Zoya Poryvayeva. And keep it. Zoya was one of my best friends in the Brigade.... What a remarkable girl! And she died a hero's death. I mean it. Many remarkable people have been killed. Those closest to me were: Zoya,[15] commander of the Brigade Arbuzov,[16] radio operator Gen'ka, Igor Glinskiy, and Grisha Shevachov. Do you realize that of the whole lot only Igor remains here? I am taking this very hard, Renochek. I intend to avenge them, motivated as I am by a terrible hatred!

Well, Renusya, I hope you'll now write to me more regularly. Kiss for me our parents very, very affectionately. Love and kisses and hugs to you too.

Ina.

Toropets, 1 September 1942

My dearest Mom!

Today I had a most unusual day: I met Daddy. Well, were we glad to meet! Admittedly, I was very upset; I find it very hard to accept that you and Reginka have been left all alone. Well, never mind! I am bound to go home for a long visit, perhaps together with Daddy.

It will no longer be just me, but both of us, Daddy and I, who will soon go on a mission, and then we'll return home to you.

But we met in such a strange manner. I had just returned from the frontier outpost, arrived in the District Committee in Toropets, and suddenly Daddy was there. So now we are celebrating our reunion!

Well, my darling, don't get upset! Don't cry! You won't? Well, that's good. Countless kisses to you, my sunshine. Please kiss Reginka for me.

Your Inka.

Fig. 7. Zoya (Masha) Poryvayeva and Georgiy Arbuzov

Undated

My tiny, dear Renok!

(No doubt, no longer so "tiny"; probably taller then Mom.) Oh, how I would love to take a look at you! Do you know how far I am from you? This letter comes to you from behind enemy lines. You've never received one like that. Ours is the usual partisan existence. Before going to sleep, you put grenades under your head and your rifle beside you; then, on waking up, you're not sure whether you'll retain the head on your shoulders. But I am confident I'll keep mine. Do you agree? Our life consists of now an ambush, now reconnaissance, now some other mission — all the time! Great! Daddy and I get along extremely well. We never argue. Quite unlike father and daughter. Really!

And you sit still there; don't keep writing to me in every letter how you envy me. Your time will come too; your life has barely begun.

Gen'ka Zaytsev had been wounded in one leg and arm, but not too badly. Renok, did Igor come to see you? Or perhaps he wrote a note to you? He had been in a hospital, and from there, it would seem, he was to go home to Kalyazin, and was to bring you my diary. Didn't he get well? How are our girls? Best wishes to them all, the very, very best!

What's new in school? When have classes begun? Well, Renok, if I survive, we'll soon see one another. Keep well, my darling little sister. Lots of love and kisses.

Your Ina.

Undated

My dear Renok!

Again, this letter comes to you "from beyond the frontier." Well, how are you, my tiny porky? For some reason, you don't write often. It will soon be a week since Daddy and I were reunited. You, Renok, ought to now help Mom in the garden, without fail. Daddy and I will come in the fall to eat your tomatoes and carrots, so you should be preparing for our visit. Don't expect us to come any sooner.

Our aircraft came yesterday; more will come today. It's they that will carry these letters. I'll likely transfer to another detachment which I like very much. I'll do my best to stay behind enemy lines; I like it here better.

After we had beaten the Germans and expelled them from here, you must come and visit the places where we fought; they are so beautiful. And we'll soon wear out the Germans.

How are you, Renochka? What's new in school? Remember me to our acquaintances. Lots of love and kisses.

Your Ina.[17]

27 September 1942

My darling!

How I love you, my darling Mom! And I am so happy to be suddenly, and against all expectations, given the opportunity to write to you! I do know how you, back home, worry about us.

Daddy and I are alive and well. We are fighting and making our contribution.[18] Admittedly, now that my best friends in the Brigade are gone (Zoya, Arbuzov, Gen'ka, and Grisha) I feel a bit out of sorts, but never mind. After all, the cause in which we are fighting is the very same as before. And even here, behind enemy lines, so close to the Germans, I feel your presence, even though you are far, far beyond the front lines...and this truly warms my heart. Daddy was made chief of intelligence at the Brigade HQ. This is not so good, but we are almost always together.

It turned cool recently, but don't worry about me. I've warm underwear and two sweaters.... Indeed, I've been toughened physically; sometimes I am exposed to rain in a marshy terrain and cold for days at a time, and nothing happens to me. I've become immune to colds, and I no longer get short-winded. I am capable of climbing any mountain now.

The beginning of our offensive has made me very happy. Well then, soon we'll defeat the enemy and again we'll be together, living a good and peaceful life. Keep well, my precious, and be happy. Don't worry about us. Love and a thousand kisses.

Your Ina.

7 November 1942

My darlings!

I would like to greet you on the occasion of the holiday and wish you the very, very best of everything!

A few days ago I sent you a postcard; since then I managed to obtain some paper and am happy to be able to write a letter to you. Very, very soon I am going to tell you [in person] everything, absolutely everything, about myself....

I returned from my assignment. I went with a section to reconnoitre a way out for the Brigade, in order to cross the front lines and get some rest. I carried out my mission, and the commander thanked me for doing a good job. I am very comfortable, resting at the home base. Here, among our boys, I feel remarkably fit. After days of fighting, it is nice to rest. I am dressed warm, am well fed, and people treat me very well.

Fateful developments are under way in our territory, and it is very pleasant for me to acknowledge that I, too, am playing a modest part in them. I lead a meaningful life, Mom. I won't have to feel ashamed of myself, after the war. And I am having a wonderful youth.

Well, my dear ones, I'll see you soon. Lots of love and kisses.

Your Ina.

8 November 1942

Hello, my darling Mom and Renok!

I am back in Soviet territory, at the home base of our Brigade, but Daddy stayed behind with the Brigade.[19] Only the reconnaissance platoon came out here, and not the entire platoon at that, a mere thirteen people.

But soon the entire Brigade will arrive here for a rest, too. In a few days, we'll go to get them. I could write a lot about this campaign and particularly the disengagement, but I've no more paper.

I feel sad; yesterday I took my very best friend to a hospital. I am so unlucky! In the meantime...I have nothing to do. Daddy commands a detachment now, and I've served in a mounted reconnaissance platoon.

You may expect me home soon. Lots of love and kisses to you both from Daddy and me. Keep well.

Your Ina.

6 December 1942

My darling Renochka!

For some reason, I haven't received any letters from you for a long, long time. Why did you stop writing? That's not nice. What's the matter? Haven't you got the time, or what?

A few days ago, I was in Toropets and sent a telegram from there, promising to be home soon, but since that time my circumstances have changed. I am most disappointed; it seems that my visit home will have to be postponed. But immediately the war ends, I'll come to stay with you for good. And now we are about to go behind enemy lines again, to join Daddy. I am so glad that I'll see him soon. At any rate, do write to me more often.

How is Mom? Kiss her for me very, very affectionately. If you only knew how I love you both! Regards to you all. Love and kisses.

Your Ina.

12 December 1942

My darling Mom!

If you only knew, my darling, how I miss you! Indeed, almost every night I dream about you and Reginka, including last night.

These are our final days of rest. Again, another mission was assigned to us, and we'll likely be gone for a long time. Well, never mind, my dear, I'll come home in the spring for sure. Perhaps even sooner. Meanwhile, you and Renochka shouldn't mope; think about us but don't worry.

I am hoping to be reunited with Daddy soon. How is he? Have you received any letters from him? We haven't had any news from the Brigade for a long time. Well, do write to me. This naughty little girl, Renka, doesn't write anything either.

We are having warm weather, and felt boots feel wet inside. And how is everything at home? Mom, please do me a favour: have your picture taken and send it to me and Daddy. OK?

Ina.

22 December 1942

My darling Mom!

Only a few more days remain until the New Year. How I always liked this holiday. And what fun I had celebrating it each year! But now I'll have to welcome the New Year under our abnormal conditions. I feel so sad, Mom! Particularly, since we are still here. And it is almost impossible now to cross over "there." Because of the offensive, the front lines have become impassable; I don't know what will become of us now.

Do you remember, Mom, the New Year a year ago? What really matters is that it is almost a year since the death of Mikhail. And I miss Misha perhaps even more than I did last year, because I now truly appreciate being alive. And still there is no news from you at home. Why is that?

My life has not changed. Kolya Dudushkin returned from the hospital; I picked him up myself. I now feel less lonely. He asked me to send you his greetings (particularly to Reginka). Well, that's all. Do write to me!

Lots of love and kisses.

Your Ina.

24 December 1942

Hello, my dear ones!

I miss you so much that I could write you every day, but when I sit down to write I don't know what to say. Well, never mind. We are now having marvellous weather; Mom would like it. It is warm and wonderful fluffy snowflakes are falling.

If only I could go home one a visit! Are my books still in one piece? Reginka has probably been hard on them. Do take good care of my books. And send me some paper, without fail; I've nothing to write on. Do write to me!

Love and kisses.

Ina.

P.S.

Mom, hurrah! We've just had news about the Brigade. All are alive and well, including Daddy. Oh, how worried I was about him; I just didn't want to write to you about this, so as not to upset you. But now all is well. We are both alive, Mom!

27 December 1942

Hello, Mom and Renok!

Yesterday I received a letter from you. If you only knew how anxious I was to get news from home! And there was a short letter from Rena at long last, about half a page.

Renochka writes that she joined the Komsomol. My congratulations. Only I was saddened by her thoughtlessness. She says: "My marks are poor, as I have no time to study." What does she mean? It appears that before she joined the Komsomol she was getting good marks, but now anything goes. Then what was the point of joining? She should not take her membership card so lightly. Others have laid down their lives for it, and she is apparently treating it as a toy. I deplore it very much.

From now in I'll not be able to send letters for some time. Only please don't worry. The mission would be completely safe. My friend Kolya Dudushkin is likely to drop in on you; he'll tell you everything about me. He is a very nice lad. Meanwhile, remember me to our relatives and friends. Lots of love and kisses.

Ina.

A LETTER TO YELENA DOROGUTINA, A GIRLFRIEND

Undated

Hello, my darling Alenka!

How nice of you to write to me! My dear "boy" with cropped hair, you have no idea how overjoyed I was to receive your letter! Only do keep writing from now on. OK? And I, too, will put all my heart and soul into keeping in touch with you.

Well, Alenushka, we are both leading genuine soldiers' lives. It is true that we are doing different things, but our lives are equally useful and worthwhile. This makes me very, very happy, Lenochka. I was saddened by your ill health. Yet you have recovered in the past and without a doubt will get well this time, too. From the bottom of my heart, I wish you a speedy and truly final recovery, so that you'll stay well.

My pussy-cat, you are the same as ever, judging by your letters.

And I, too, live well. Remarkably well! I am a partisan, serving in a mounted reconnaissance platoon. I learned to prance on a horse like a true cavalryman, and I grew very attached to my Grey. I am a fairly good shot; I won several sharpshooting prizes. I am toughened, and have grown stronger in body and spirit. Do you remember when we were in Grade 9? What wonderful times we had!

Well, Lenushka, it is getting dark and I must end. Love and kisses and hugs to you, my dear little friend. Write to me directly to my unit, since I am leaving Kashin in a few days.

More kisses.

Your Ina.

NOTES

1.   Party representative and co-commander in the Red Army, empowered to overrule his military commander in case of need. The appointment was created in 1918, for the purpose of ensuring the loyalty of commanders. On 9 October 1942 military commissars in the regular army were replaced by the less powerful political deputy commanders, in the cause of efficiency. However, an exception was made regarding partisan units as a means of maintaining morale and discipline. See *Sovetskaya Voyennaya Entsyklopediya* [Soviet Military Encyclopedia], III, 301-302; V. Perezhogin, "O komissarakh partizanskikh formirovaniy [About the Commissars of Partisan Formations]," *Voyenno-istoricheskiy zhurnal* [Journal of Military History], No. 4 (1978), pp. 101-107.

2.   Georgiy Arbuzov, Commander of the 2nd Kalinin Partisan Brigade. Petr Lekomtsev, the third man, was in fact head of the Brigade's Political Section (Party organ charged with morale building and indoctrination). This was a staff appointment, in contrast to that of "commissar," a line officer. However, under partisan conditions the distinction was less clear. Lekomtsev eventually replaced the Brigade Commissar Abramov when the latter was recalled by the Kalinin Front (Army Group) HQ. See N.V. Masolov, *Ballada o krasnom desante* [A Ballad About the Red Airborne Assault Force] (Moscow: Politizdat, 1967), pp. 25, 157.

3.   While Arbuzov, Khrustalev, Lekomtsev, and Konstantinova drove westward to the village of Kuvshinovo, having left Kalinin on 9 June, Khrustalev told humorous war stories on the way. Arbuzov commented on them, citing various proverbs. Ina laughed a lot. Even the usually serious Lekomtsev was amused. See Masolov, *Ballada*, p. 25.

4.   "My hand will never falter, when aiming the weapon at the enemy," said Ina and unexpectedly burst out crying. During one of the halts, Arbuzov called Ina "comrade" (a formal address) for the first and last time. Subsequently, he was always addressing her in an informal and friendly manner. See Masolov, *Ballada*, p. 26.

5.   The names of the interpreter and radio operator were Vasiliy Mochalov and Gennadiy Nikitin respectively. Two of the scouts were young women Dusya Tsvetova and Zoya (real name, Mariya — diminutive, Masha) Poryvaycva, who had both undergone "special" training. See Masolov, *Ballada*, p. 27.

6.   On the third day, Arbuzov's party reached Ostashkov. Here he turned in a south-westerly direction, toward Moscow — Riga Railroad. Meanwhile, Ina kept asking endless questions, which Tsvetova and Poryvayeva tried to answer. They taught her how to prepare meals and roll up bedding quickly. The group reached Kunya, 30 kilometres from the front lines, on 16 June. See Masolov, *Ballada*, pp. 28, 35.

7.   Soviet troops regained a number of districts in Kalinin Region during the winter of 1941-42. Advancing along the boundaries between the German Army Groups "North" and "Centre," in a forested, swampy terrain with a lot of lakes and infrequent roads, and negotiating snow up to 1-1/2 metres deep, the Soviet 4th Shock Army took the town of Toropets by storm. On the other hand, the 3rd Shock Army, fighting along an almost 250 kilometre front, reached the strategically important railroad triangle formed by the stations of Velikiye Luki, Nevel', and Novosokol'niki. But it couldn't overcome enemy resistance on the shores of the Lovat' River. Here the front was stabilized until the fall of 1943. See Masolov, *Ballada*, pp. 18-19.

8.   One of the three detachments forming part of the 2nd Kalinin Partisan Brigade commanded by Georgiy Arbuzov. (The other detachments were those commanded by Ryndin and Shipovalov respectively.) The origins of the Brigade were as follows:

The HQ of the Partisan Movement was set up in September 1941 as a civilian (Party) central partisan control agency. (See Howell, *The Soviet Partisan Movement, 1941-1944*, p. 65.)

By the early spring of 1942, the Kalinin Party Regional Committee and the army HQ of the Kalinin Front (Army Group) became convinced that there was a need to intensify action behind enemy lines in aid of the regular army. On 24 March 1942, the Kalinin Party Regional Committee's Bureau adopted a decision on "Measures to develop a partisan movement in the Region." In Kalinin and other towns, small, well-armed units were formed, which operated in the war zone in the Velikiye Luki, Nevel', and Novosokol'niki triangle, interfering with the enemy supply system.

Around that time, the 2nd (Leningrad) Special Brigade returned from its deep raid in the direction of the old Latvian border. The first Soviet partisan brigade of World War II, this unit originated as the "brain child" of Lieutenant-General N.F. Vatutin, chief of staff of the North-Western Front (Army Group) and Colonel K.N. Derevyanko, his chief of intelligence. The unit was led by Major Aleksey Litvinenko (nicknamed "Red Cossack" and mistaken by the Germans for a general). His chief of intelligence was Senior Lieutenant (later on, Captain) Aleksandr German, a gifted legendary Soviet partisan leader. The Brigade consisted of only 400 horsemen and 20 carts. Its success indicated that raiding was the right partisan tactic in the north-west.

The command element of the 2nd Shock Army suggested that another raid, modelled on the one carried out by 2nd Special Brigade, be undertaken by the Kalinin partisans. It was decided to form a small, mobile brigade, to be sent to the distant rear of the German 18th Army encircling Leningrad, in the vicinity of Idritsa and Pustoshka. (This last was the newest town of the then western Kalinin Region, built at the crossing of Moscow — Riga Railroad and Kiev — Leningrad Highway. Before the war it was a centre of a large agricultural district, bordering on Latvia. Its roads were of strategic importance to the enemy who invaded the area in the first half of July 1941. There was no time to organize a Party underground or irregular fighting groups beforehand, and a large concentration of enemy troops in the first few months of the war made it difficult to do so at that time. After the invasion, some underground groups came into being here in the fall, organized mainly by Red Army men and some local teachers.)

The objectives of the participants in the second raid (who were to be mistaken by the Germans for an airborne assault force) were: recon-naissance along the roads, acts of sabotage, agitation among the populace, and the creation of new centres of resistance. The majority in the Brigade were to be students: girls and boys aged seventeen to eighteen. See Masolov, *Ballada*, pp. 21-22, 96, 98; *Neobychnyy reid* [Unusual Raid] (Moscow: Politizdat, 1972).

9.   Kupuy was a large village, located on the Lovat' River, 13 kilometres from the city of Velikiye Luki. (This historic city in Pskov Region has stood on the Lovat' River for 800 years, guarding the distant approaches to Moscow. The Velikiye Luki bridgehead saw fierce fighting during World War II. Thrown back from Moscow, German troops held onto the bridgehead and considerably strengthened it in the spring of 1942. The front lines passed near the city's ancient walls, along the river.) It was here, in the village of Kupuy,

that the 2nd Kalinin Brigade was formed. Ina was assigned to a detachment of the Brigade which was formed first; its commander was Lieutenant Petr Ryndin.

Other members of the detachment who arrived in the assembly area before Ina did reached Kupuy in three stages. On 18 April 1942 the group boarded a train in Kalinin. On their arrival in Ostashkov, they drilled there for eight days. Then they boarded another train for Toropets, where they were outfitted and received supplies. The last stage of the trip had to be accomplished on foot in field service marching order. It took four days. There were a number of girls who were unaccustomed to army boots and developed blisters on their feet. But none of them complained or demanded a prolonged rest. See Masolov, *Ballada*, pp. 20-21, 37-39.

10.   The first mission executed by eight partisans from Ryndin's detachment was apparently successful. The partisans stayed in three villages behind enemy lines. Although their inhabitants were frightened, some were eager to fight. Eight individuals went on the mission, but more than twenty came back. The new recruits had arms of their own. In the first half of June the detachment fulfilled several missions, involving the mining of the Leningrad — Riga Railroad, gathering intelligence on German military units and supplies, and collecting weapons. The detachment "explored" the Nevel' and Velikiye Luki Districts, and partially the Novosokol'niki and Pustoshka Districts as well. (The missions were of few days duration each; the operations area was located 60-70 kilometres from Kupuy.) The detachment's mines exploded as far as Pustoshka, along the ancient Kiev — Leningrad Highway. Similar tactics were employed by Lesnikov's and Shipovalov's detachments. The latter was most effective; its personnel were former Red Army soldiers who had broken out of encirclement and were experienced saboteurs. See Masolov, *Ballada*, p. 42.

In the summer of 1942, when the German army was advancing in the south, the Kalinin partisans mined railroads and highways on a mass scale, thus interfering with the transfer of men and equipment from the northwestern sectors of the front to the Volga (Stalingrad) sector and the Caucasus. Since 15 June 1942, the partisans in the Kalinin Region were controlled by the HQ of the Partisan Movement, attached to the Military Council of the Kalinin Front (Army Group), which assumed full control over the partisan formations in the Front's zone, including partly the Smolensk Region and Belorussia as well. See N.I. Makarov, "Po zovu Rodiny [Summoned by the Homeland]," in *Sovetskiye partizany* [Soviet Partisans], V.Ye Bystrov, ed. (Moscow: Gospolitizdat, 1963), pp. 96, 97.

11.   The Brigade crossed the front lines without firing a single shot. The next night the Brigade executed a forced march from Novosokol'niki District to Pustoshka District, and reached the village of Linets, 10 kilometres from Pustoshka, along the Kiev — Leningrad Highway. Here Arbuzov assigned missions to three scouts: Dusya, Zoya, and Ina. See Masolov, *Ballada*, pp. 99-101.

12.   The last two undated letters were written much earlier than 2 August, and appear in the original published text out of their proper chronological sequence, since the evidence suggests that Ina's illness occurred before the Brigade's transfer behind enemy lines on 30 July, following which, on 3 August, Ina and Zoya went on their fateful missions; both were caught by the enemy, but Ina managed to escape.

13.   The real name of "Zoya" was Masha (Mariya) Poryvayeva. Ina's mission was to reconnoitre the garrisons of Idritsa, Alol', and Pustoshka. See Minayeva, *et al.*, eds., *Srazhalas*, p. 11.

14.   Contrary to her expectations, Ina at first had a lot of luck. Attempting to reach Kiev — Leningrad Highway, she met an old woman in a glade covered with ripe strawberries. Ina learned from the woman, through a careful choice of questions, what was the safest way to reach the small town of Alol'. Walking through a thick fir and pine forest, along an unused trail and then through a clearing, Ina reached the town's hospital.

The first person she met was a tall man of about fifty, who replied politely to her greeting and apologized for having to examine her passport. It turned out that it was Ivan Korobovskiy, the Alol' Rural District elder, a collaborator who had betrayed a number of partisans. However, Ina's calm and child-like naivety deceived him. When she learned of the man's identity, Ina decided to leave the settlement as soon as possible. Before doing so, however, she managed to get information on the German punitive detachment based nearby, in the village of Nochlegovo. She walked along the highway to Pustoshka and stopped for the night before reaching her destination, having reconnoitred the security of the bridge across the Krupiya River in the village of Slobodka.

Preoccupied with the spectre of the "Red Airborne Assault Force," the army of occupation relaxed its vigilance in Pustoshka. This enabled Ina to collect a lot of important information. She felt great and was anxious to rejoin the Brigade. When she noted a large column of trucks filled with soldiers at the railroad crossing, the temptation to find out where they were going was too great. So she was arrested. She was taken from the Kommendatura by truck to the town of Idritsa. There, at the field gendarmerie, a grey-haired, flabby Nazi captain listened to her "story" indifferently, smiled crookedly, and called a soldier to escort Ina back to Pustoshka, handing him some papers. Thus Ina fell into clutches of the infamous Wagner, chief of the *Geheime Feldpolizei*, who interrogated her through a certain Vikentiy Svirida, the son of a White Russian émigré. See Masolov, *Ballada*, pp. 105-107.

Ina managed to run away again. After covering a distance of several kilometres, she stopped for a rest in a forest, by a remote stream. She was thirsty and drank a lot of water. As she rested, stretched out beside a hazelnut bush, she gradually came to the conclusion that she must immediately attempt to reach the front lines and then cross into Soviet territory. She thus made the only correct decision possible under the circumstances, based on the following considerations.

Unaware of Poryvayeva's capture near the village of Shchukino but suspecting that her own arrest and flight were known in settlements of Kopylka, Alol', and Slobodka, all located near Shchukino, Ina decided to run in the opposite direction. She was aware that in order to reach the forest north-west of Shchukino, the temporary location of the Brigade, she would have had to make a very large detour. Consequently, it would have taken her about five days to reach the Brigade on foot. However, the Brigade was not likely to wait for her this long. On the other hand, the intelligence she had obtained was interesting and new, and could prove useful to her superiors in the near future. Ina resolutely got up and walked eastward. Four days later, walking along a familiar path, she reached a partisan crossing place on the Lovat'. See Masolov, *Ballada*, p. 110.

15. While on a regular reconnaissance mission near Shchukino (as mentioned above) Poryvayeva was caught on or about 5 August 1942, tortured, and executed.

The assumption of the name "Zoya" by Poryvayeva, a former worker of an accordion factory in Moscow, was doubly symbolic. It implied the notion of sacrifice so that others may live ("Zoya" means "life" in Greek). Also "Zoya" happened to be the name of Zoya Kosmodem'yanskaya, the most famous Soviet schoolgirl-partisan, hanged by the Germans during the Battle of Moscow. The poignant story of Masha Poryvayeva is told by Masolov in his *Tayna Zoi Kruglovoy* [The Secret of Zoya Kruglova] (Leningrad: Lenizdat, 1962), pp. 3-22, and in his *Ballada*, passim. See also Minayeva, *et al.*, eds., *Srazhalas'*, p. 9n.

16. Arbuzov was killed on 13 August 1942 during the fighting with a German punitive detachment from Nochlegovo, which took place some 13 kilometres from the town of Opochka in Alol' Forest. He was about

30-years-old. Petr Ryndin replaced him as commander of the Brigade. Both held the army rank of Senior Lieutenant. See Masolov, *Ballada*, pp. 133-46.

17.   The contents of Ina's two undated letters addressed to her sister Rena, which appear in the original after the letter of 27 September 1942, indicate that they had been written earlier. Therefore, I placed them immediately ahead of this letter.

18.   The 1st Kalinin Partisan Corps, in which Ina served with her father, was formed in Kupuy in the late summer of 1942. Its objectives were: to penetrate deep behind enemy lines; disrupt enemy communications; blow up rail junctions and bridges; destroy enemy stores, garrisons, police formations, installations, and administrative agencies; and recruit able-bodied population of both sexes. See Masolov, *Ballada*, pp. 152-53; Makarov, in *Sovetskiye partizany*, p. 98.

On 4 September, the Corps, numbering about 3,000, advanced along the road reconnoitred by the 2nd Kalinin Partisan Brigade, which marched in the Corps' advance party. "Bridges and rails shot up, trains were derailed, and trucks blew up on highways." Many a Nazi garrison ceased to exist. Hundreds joined the ranks. "The ground burned under the feet of the invaders.... For six hundred days the flame of the people's war was to rage on the shores of the Velikaya and Issa rivers, near Pustoshka and Sebezh, by Idritsa and Opochka." See Masolov, *Ballada*, p. 153.

19.   After fulfilling its mission, the 1st Kalinin Partisan Corps was reorganized at the end of October. Henceforward, the brigade became the largest partisan unit in the area. Each brigade was attached to a district to facilitate the execution of its military and political tasks. First Party secretaries in such districts became brigade commissars. See Makarov, in *Sovetskiye partizany*, p. 100.

THE DIARY AND LETTERS OF INA KONSTANTINOVA

(Partisan: 1943-1944)

4 February 1943

My dear Mom!

Well, I had a good trip and here I am in Moscow. [Ina spent the period between 2 January and 3 February 1943 at home on leave.] I went to see Aunt Tonya, and we just returned from the movies. We saw my favourite film *The Oppenheim Family* The first thing I did was to request a long distance telephone conversation with you. My darling, so I'll hear your voice once more.... Don't be sad, don't cry. You know, I am bound to come back soon. I know it, I feel it.

Remember me to Grandmother and kiss Reginka for me.

Your Ina.

7 February 1943

Hello, my dear Mom!

It was only today that I managed to get through to you. I am going away on Tuesday, but already I am a bit bored in Moscow. I went to the cinema and the Hermitage. I very much liked the film entitled *The Invincible Ones*, about life in Leningrad. Have your written to me? How is Grandmother? How is Rena? Today I am planning to see the play entitled *Kremlin Chimes* at the Artistic Theatre.

Well, that's all for now. Remember me to Grandmother, Rena, and our acquaintances. Lots of love and kisses to you.

Ina.

8 February 1943

My dear Mom!

Yesterday I talked to you on the telephone, and tomorrow I plan to do this again. My darling, I enjoy hearing you dear voice so!

I went to the Artistic yesterday and saw *Kremlin Chimes*. A remarkable play! Do you know that Livanov was one of the actors? He portrayed Dubrovskiy in the movies. People are crazy about him; I am too.

Soon I must go to the station to find out about the train for tomorrow. Again, I'll travel in an upholstered car. Well, my dearest, that's all for now. Kiss Reginka and Grandmother for me.

I wish you all the very, very best. Lots of love and kisses.

Your Ina.

9 February 1943.

Hello, my dear Mom, Grandmother, and Reginka!

Today I am leaving Moscow; it's high time for me to do it. I spent almost a week here. My train leaves in the evening. I've time to go to a hairdresser. I am so sorry I couldn't have my photo taken — on account of a sore eye. Well, never mind; it's healing already.

Aunt Tonya stuffed all kinds of food in my kit-bag; it'll be heavy to carry. Yesterday I went to the movies to see *Sixty Days.*

Well, that's all. I'll write to you next from Bologoye. And, in the meantime, love to you all. Keep well.

Your Ina.

16 February 1943

My darling!

Here I am, finally, at the home base. I'll describe my trip, one thing at a time. I left Moscow on the 9th and on the 10th I reached Bologoye. I was told that there would be a long wait for the train to Toropets, and I spent the night in a sleeping-car. I was very comfortable, cozy and warm, and my bedding was soft. The next day I managed to catch a troop train. I was invited to travel in one of the several coaches occupied by a large party of airmen; I was given the most comfortable spot, on a top bunk near the stove, and had a very good trip.

On the 15th I reached Toropets. I sent you a telegram and left for the base. I inquired of a certain official concerning Daddy's whereabouts. He said that there were no losses among the command personnel of our brigade (as had been announced on the radio). When I arrived, nobody from our group was at the base. I am planning to start out tomorrow, to try to catch up with the detachments, but I don't know whether I would be successful. So I might not be able to cross behind enemy lines for a while. Our commander Tyapin and one girl are here; he wants to send the two of us back to school. Well, that's all for now. Love to you all.

Your Ina.

19 February 1943

Hello, my dear Mom, Grandmother, and Renochka!

I am writing to you from the Tactical HQ. Yesterday I had a talk with a lieutenant-colonel. In a few days I'll join Daddy.

Don't worry about me; the crossing will be very well-organized. I feel very well and am ready to go. Probably I won't be able to write to you any more. In the meantime, lots of love and kisses.

Your Ina.

Undated

My dear Mom!

Here I am finally reunited with Daddy. Well, what's there to say about him? He looks great. Much better than before.

I haven't got the time to finish this letter, because the plane is about to take off. I have time only to implore you: don't worry.

Your Ina.

1 April 1943

My dear Renochka!

It is already a long time since I left home, and I miss you a great deal, especially since we are still stuck here, and I don't know when it would be possible for us to go "there."[1]

I've changed my duty, but at the earliest opportunity I'll return to mounted reconnaissance. Meanwhile, I deliver secret parcels to brigades. There are ten of us; we work in pairs. I was ordered to accompany Senior-Lieutenant Yusupov.

There are five officers and five messengers. The lads are very nice, but it's too bad that I am the only girl in the group.

Well, and what's new with you? How are you doing in school? Do write to me, my little "dragon-fly."

Remember me to Mom and Grandmother. Love and kisses.

Your Ina.

21 April 1943

Hello, my dear ones!

Again, there is a possibility of getting a letter through to you, and again Daddy and I are writing to you. Considerable changes have taken place in our lives.

First of all, we are no longer in the reconnaissance detachment, but have transferred to another district, to another detachment of our brigade. Daddy now serves as deputy brigade commander, but no one knows what my function is. My undefined status is burdensome to me, and I am constantly asking to be transferred back to the platoon.

This detachment is very nice, at least at first sight. We live well. I now carry a submachine gun and feel very important.

My dear ones, your letters mean so much to me. How are you? How is Renochka doing in school? I've a feeling that having a good time is more important to her now. Meanwhile, I would dearly love to be back in school!

Here summer is already approaching. The snow has gone, the ground is dry everywhere, and the weather is warm. Soon May Day will come. From the bottom of my heart, I wish you the best possible holiday. Keep well.... Write to me more often.

Lots of love and kisses.

Your Ina.

Undated

Hello, my dearest Mom!

I don't know when it would be possible to send you this letter. In short, I miss you very much.

My darling Mom, this fall I must go back to school.

We are still together, Daddy and I. Recently our brigade, among others, was engaged in heavy fighting; it was surrounded, but broke out of the encirclement with its honour intact. The losses in the Brigade were relatively low.[2] Daddy and I now serve in another detachment.

Mom, my sunshine, how I would love to receive even the shortest note from you, even a few lines! And there is not the slightest hope for this to happen. Well, how are you my dear ones? Without a doubt, you have had a lot of hardships to endure this spring.

Love and countless kisses to you both. Greetings from Daddy. Here is another kiss from me.

Your Ina.

15 June 1943

My darling Mom!

Finally, I've the occasion to write you a detailed letter about myself. I warn you it will be long. First of all, because of the cool weather, we are now stationed in a village. I am working in reconnaissance and often go on missions. An entire garrison went over to us recently, and I am glad that I, too, contributed to this. A few days ago, our saboteurs derailed a train.

On the third day, one lad and I rode about 20 km.... We had such fun! Earlier, a long time ago, I was quite sick and felt rotten. I caused Dad a great deal of worry, but I managed to pull through.[3]

My last wound has skinned over, and I am now in perfect health. Again, I ride my horse, at a spanking pace, through these marvellous woods. We plan to go swimming, when the weather warms up. What a beautiful river!

By and large, I lead a good life. The detachment is well disposed toward me. I've many good friends here. Dad and I get along fine; only I see him very seldom. Apparently, he is busy; well, you know what he is like. He looks highly presentable, but very homesick.

It is now evening, and we are truly enjoying it. Daddy is relaxing with a book and I feel homesick so I decided to write to you, my dear Mom. This a very beautiful country, with forests all around, where nightingales keep singing at night, and so loud at that.... And the nights are moonlit and bright. I should be home not later than August, in order to attend the Institute in the fall. Don't expect me before then. I lead a very, very good life, a life for real. And I am so fond of all of its aspects: the woods, nights, ambushes, comrades, Voronka [the horse], and serving alongside Daddy.

Well, and how are you, my dear ones? How are you managing? What are you doing? Your last letters were dated February; for some reason, we haven't been receiving any mail recently. I visualize our garden so clearly: Mom behind the beds and Reginka with pails of water. And then Mom goes to bed, alone in the house, of course, because Reginka is out, and Mom is thinking about us. And we, too, think about both of you every night. Well, here is the end of my sheet.

Remember us to our acquaintances, teachers, and everyone else.

Cover Reginka with kisses for me. Love and kisses and hugs to you, my dear. On Daddy's behalf too.

Your Ina.

LETTERS TO NYURA PUDELEVA

13 August 1943

My dearest Nyurka!

Well, of course, I am going to reply to your letter. What is more, I would have written to you first had I known your address. You see, I had written to you some time ago. Haven't you received any of my letters?

My dear Nyura, your letter exudes something so homey and so wonderful, albeit belonging to a very distant past. We haven't seen each other for such a long time, and these two years have changed both of us a great deal. This was inevitable. Well, all the same I am convinced that when we meet again we'll recapture the kinship and closeness which we used to share, and which, apart from Lyusya, I had not experienced with anyone else. I now lead the kind of life I dreamed of: a soldier's life, active and for real. Admittedly, I am awfully sorry it is coming to an end. That is, not my life, but this kind of life. I am doing quite well, apparently. My superiors appreciate my service; I have been serving in a reconnaissance platoon from the beginning, and am now an expert scout. I carry a sub-machine gun and a pistol, and I ride Mashka, a nice, fiery little mare. In no respect I am inferior to our lads; in fact, on the contrary, the commander often singles me out as an example to follow.

I am proud of this, Nyurok.

My personal score now stands at fifteen Germans killed.

I'll soon go to Moscow to study. Consequently, it is not unlikely that we'll soon see one another.

I am waiting for an aircraft, in order to cross the front; I am writing to you from a partisan district, far behind enemy lines.

Best regards to you from Dad; we are here together.

Well, Nyurok, I await a detailed letter from you about everything that concerns you. Write to me, my dear. Meanwhile, lots of love and kisses to you.

Your Ina.

27 August 1943

My dear Nyurok!

I sent you a letter recently, but I am not sure that it'll reach you, since a lot of mail went up in flames when our airfield was bombed. Indeed, we are frequently being bombed here. Recently bombers overflew the dispositions of our brigade.[4]

I am not too happy right now. I've been discharged from an operational detachment, and I sit here waiting for an aircraft to fly me out to Soviet territory, but it is taking so long to come. Or to be more precise, some aircraft did come but not the one I am waiting for. Yet I believe that in a few days the matter will be settled one way or another. Either the plane will finally come to get me, or I'll return to my detachment.

Well, how are you? What's new with you? Write me everything but everything about yourself.

Nyurok, I wish we were reunited soon, so that we could talk; there is so much to talk about! Write to me to my home address. Meanwhile, love and kisses to you.

Your Ina.

INA'S LETTERS TO HER FAMILY

27 August 1943

Hello, my dear ones!

I haven't written to you for a long time, hoping that we'll be soon reunited, but sometimes things don't turn out according to our wishes. I've already spent a month in this partisan territory, to which I came in order to fly out to you. I've finalized all the formalities with the command personnel, I've been ready to leave for a long time, and the aircraft keep flying, but my guide has not yet returned from beyond the front lines. I am waiting and waiting, and still there is no sign of him. And it is extremely difficult now to cross the front lines.

Here I am waiting for the impossible to happen.

And how are you? Write to me, anyway; perhaps the mail will reach me. Has the school year begun yet? How is school? How is the garden? Probably food is now easier to obtain for you. Here we worry about your food situation, but we can't help you.

Every night, before going to bed, Daddy reminisces about everything at home. We lead a good life; Daddy looks well. Possibly, he will come home on leave this winter.

Since I finished my work in the detachment and came here, I've also gained weight and am now almost as plump as when I was home, during the winter.

Write to me more often. Well, love and kisses and hugs to you, my darlings,

Your Ina.

Undated

My darlings:

A few days ago I received the following order from the Brigade Commander: Daddy is wanted in Belorussia. I ought to accompany him, but it would be more convenient to stay here, in the detachment, and therefore Daddy and I will part for the time being, but hopefully not for very long.

I live well. Don't worry about me. After all, I'll return home to you soon. Did Mom send my matriculation certificate to the Aircraft Design Institute, as requested? I am hoping to study next year. My dear ones, every night, before going to sleep, we talk about you.... From now on I'll think about you even more often than before.

And how handsome our Daddy is, Mom! Honest, it would be difficult to find someone better looking than him. He is now wearing German riding breeches, a field shirt with crimson collar tabs, a leather double-breasted jacket, and an officer's cloak. In addition, he has a good Belgian pistol and an officer's sword-belt. So, with his head of hair, he looks most impressive. He was recommended for yet another decoration. Everyone treats him with respect, and I am very proud of him.[5]

I, too, am well treated here. I am valued as a good soldier and scout. So you needn't blush on account of me.[6]

Daddy will write to you from Belorussia about everything.

Well, my dear ones, lots of love and kisses and hugs to you.

Ina.

Undated

Hello, my dear Daddy!

First of all, we reached our destination safely. I found the detachment unchanged. I work in reconnaissance in the same section.

And how is everything? Any news? What is happening in the Brigade? Have you received any letters? How is my Mishka? Daddy, perhaps the occupation of Nevel' has had some effect on the situation in the Partisan Territory? Explain, otherwise it is difficult for me to make sense of what's happening.[7]

Please send me a Shpagin submachine gun cartridge; get it from Tokarev and, if possible, also obtain 3 to 4 metres of parachute harness for saddle-girth and stirrups. Only don't you forget it; send them to me without fail. Well, my dear, I'll expect a letter from you and the other things.

If aircraft are flying, and often at that, write to me, as the letters will reach me. Meanwhile, lots of love and kisses to you. Remember me to Commissar Vanyusha.

All the best to you.

Your Ina.

16 December 1943

My dear ones!

Today I re-read your letters and decided to write to you myself. Only, for some reason, I haven't received anything from you for a long, long time. Why aren't you writing? Have you disowned me? Look here, don't you forget me.

I am still here. My situation is unchanged. I am tired of resting; I am impatient to be back in action!

Daddy remains in the rear.[8] I hope we'll be reunited soon. Well, lots of love and kisses to you.

Your Ina.

21 February 1944

My dear Mom!

I've written an entire series of letters to you. After all, it's been already five months since I've received any news from you, and you, too, are not getting any letters. And do you realize, Mom, how homesick I am, how I miss you. My darling! In the early morning, the commander wakes me up to go reconnoitring. I wake up and remember how, long time ago, my nanny woke me up to go to school. I didn't want to get up, I wanted to have a long lie in the warm bed, but now it's so different.... I walk in the woods in the morning, thinking and remembering.... Particularly when I have been left all alone.

Where is Daddy right now? Is he with you?

My darling, I'll finish the next day. "All clear" has just been given and we again settle in our bunkers.

We are now experiencing cold weather here. Probably, it is cold at home, too. In my mind's eye, I see the frost-fashioned flowery patterns on the windows of my room; I see our home, so pleasant and full of sunshine.

In a week it will be a year since I arrived here.

Mom, do you know that, for the past few days, for some reason the sound of the war zone's cannonade is no longer heard, and war communiqués don't gladden either. To make up for it, how our aircraft keep the Germans busy in good weather!

The enemy has grown completely decrepit. Lately, punitive expeditions ar sent against the partisans frequently. But our losses are relatively low.

I heard a rumour here that Dad had been appointed Secretary of the Pustoshka District Committee. He'll find his duties very difficult. After all, there is so much to do here! I know the local population, and I can visualize the working conditions. This is not Kashin. It would not be a bad idea for him to stay in Kashin. Also, this is not a good place to bring one's family to live.

Well, and how is Reginka doing in school? It seems to me that our top student is slipping. Of course, she is loaded with community work, as usual. I've such an urge to cover her with kisses....

Well this is the end of the sheet.

Good-bye for now. Wait for me. And in the meantime all the best to you. Love and kisses.

Your silly, very silly Ina.

25 February 1944

My dear Mom!

Finally, it is possible to arrange the delivery of this letter to you. How many letters I have written, even though I knew beforehand that you won't receive them! During difficult moments I had the urge to share my thoughts with you somehow, and I kept writing. All these letters are now in my knapsack.

Well, what's there to say.

I am alive, well, and equipped with clothing and footwear. Most of all, I long for the arrival of our troops.

The front is very, very near, and still they haven't come.[9] Meanwhile, I rejoice at every bomb dropped by our aircraft, at every Soviet shell fired.

Countless kisses to you, my dear ones. Wait for me; do wait for me.

Your Ina.

* * *

This was Ina's final letter. No more letters or entries in her diary had been found.

NOTES

1.   "There" refers to the "Partisan Territory." The growing strength of the partisans and support of the population made it possible to create a "Partisan Territory" behind enemy lines and restore Soviet administration there. At first, the Territory included the southern parts of Pustoshka, Idritsa, and Sebezh Districts. Then the northern parts of Sebezh and Idritsa Districts

also fell to the partisans, as well as the southern part of the Opochka District. The creation of the Partisan Territory in Kalinin Region was facilitated by the existence of a similar territory in Belorussia, in Rossony, Osveya, and Drissa Districts bordering on Kalinin Region. The area liberated by Kalinin and Belorussian partisans stretched for 100 kilometres from east to west and 80-90 kilometres from north to south. See Makarov, in *Sovetskiye partizany*, p. 100.

2.   The enemy, anxious to abolish the Partisan Territory, kept sending punitive expeditions against it, armed with tanks, artillery, and aircraft. Yet the partisans initially managed not only to repel the attacks, but even to increase the area they occupied. See Makarov, in *Sovetskiye partizany*, pp. 104-105.

3.   Ina's illness is described in detail by her father (see p. 99).

4.   Between August and November 1943, the enemy systematically bombed the Partisan Territory and its settlements, to interfere with the harvesting of crops, deprive the partisans of supply bases and living quarters for the winter, and turn the population against them. But they failed to achieve their main objective: to crush the resistance of both the partisans and the peasants. The Territory continued to exist until the arrival of the Red Army in November 1943. See Makarov, in *Sovetskiye partizany*, p. 105.

5.   Contrary to the arrangement in the original text, this letter as well as the next one should precede rather than follow Ina's letter of 16 December. Their content indicates that both were written before Ina's father was wounded and evacuated to Soviet-held territory. See Note 8.

6.   In 1943-44 Ina executed dozens of missions, carrying out very difficult and risky assignments. She took part in the fighting, ambushes of enemy sol-diers, and acts of sabotage. See Makarov, in *Sovetskiye partizany*, p. 118; Minayeva, *et al.*, eds., *Srazhalas*, p. 11.

7.   On 7 October 1943 the troops of the Kalinin Front (Army Group) under the command of Army General A.I. Yeremenko captured Nevel', a major centre of enemy resistance, as well as many other settlements. Now the front lines ran only 30-35 kilometres from the eastern boundary of the Partisan Territory. At the beginning of November, the troops of the 2nd Baltic Front (Army Group) advanced from the vicinity of Nevel' toward the Partisan Territory, but the enemy managed to stop them, concentrating large regular units along the frontiers of the Territory and intensively bombing its settlements. The intensified attacks against the Partisan Territory resulted in cutting it almost in half, from north to south. The front lines here remained stabilized right up to July 1944, along a line running from Dretun' through Neshchedrovo Lake to Pustoshka. See Makarov, in *Sovetskiye partizany*, pp. 114-15.

8.   In November 1943 Ina's father was wounded and evacuated to a rear hospital.

9.   As a result of enemy reprisals, the partisans had to abandon their villages and live in the forest. Thousands of peasants with their personal effects and cattle followed them. Eventually, the conditions under which the partisans existed became extremely difficult. They now operated near the front lines or on them and, as a result, were constantly harassed and forced to keep changing their camps. Between December 1943 and June 1944, nineteen large punitive expeditions, unprecedented in earlier periods, were sent against them. Short of food and clothing, the partisans had to deal with the numerically superior, well armed and well supplied enemy, who now initiated battles in the open during which the partisans were placed at distinct disadvantage. The punitive expeditions levelled villages with the ground, seized peasant property, and killed the inhabitants, or sent them to Germany as slave labour. Thus the partisans were deprived of their supply bases. On the other hand, they were now supplied by air from Soviet rear areas only sporadically, due to poor weather and frequent enemy punitive actions. Moreover, the large number of the sick and wounded among the partisans adversely affected their mobility. The situation deteriorated even further in the spring, due to the growing intensity of German punitive operations. See Makarov, in *Sovetskiye partizany*, pp. 115-16.

THE STORY OF A DAUGHTER

A. Konstantinov

Our troop train was approaching the station at Toropets. We hastily unloaded our weapons, equipment, and food supplies. Then we quickly put everything in a pile and covered it with raincapes. I was impatient to go downtown and to find Khrustalev, the Party Regional Committee official, in order to determine Ina's whereabouts.

Unexpectedly, I ran into Khrustalev on my way to the District Committee. I handed him my order, assigning me to the 2nd Partisan Brigade. He anticipated my question by saying: "Let us both look for your daughter!"

"What do you mean?"

"Well, she learned that in a few days the Brigade will cross behind enemy lines. So she secretly left the Tactical HQ yesterday, having interrupted her convalescence."

We rushed to the District Committee. We rang up the frontier outposts. Nobody knew anything. I made the rounds of the frontier regiments' HQs located in the town. Finally, late in the evening I learned that Ina was being held at a frontier command post about 35 kilometres from Toropets, but the communication with the outpost was broken. I ordered a saddle horse for the following morning, and I made it to the District Committee as early as 0500 hours. I waited impatiently for the horse, and it was nowhere to be found. I sent a messenger to the base.

It was 0900 hours! I impatiently paced up and down the huge assembly hall of the District Committee, in which the partisan assembly point was located. The door opened and suddenly I saw Inka, wearing a black beret, white blouse, and big boots.

"Daddy!"

Like a whirlwind, she threw herself at me, hugging, kissing me, and asking hundreds of questions. Here she was before me, my little daughter: tanned, a bit coarser looking, slightly thinner, but for all that just as merry, cheerful, and restless as she ever was.

I could hardly keep up with her, answering her questions. Suddenly, on her right hand I noticed a big, dry scab, and the slight swelling of her fingers.

"What's that, Ina?"

"Nothing much; I'll tell you about it later. And you...how long will you stay?"

"I am here for good."

She kept looking at me for a while, saying nothing, then she started to hug me, kiss me, and pull me about.

"I am so glad you are here! Only please don't be foolish and go straight home. How will Mom manage by herself? And you'll cause me extra trouble, too." She assumed a worried look. "But Daddy, this is not Kashin — not even the Civil War — this is something more serious," she told me in a preaching tone.

"Well, well, never mind. Really, I'll try to adjust somehow so as not to cause you too much trouble," I replied in a tone that was just as serious, but I had a hard time trying not to burst our laughing.

"Well, really, what am I to do with you now?" she said pensively.

"First of all, my little girl...."

"Daddy, I am no longer a little girl, but a scout of 2nd Kalinin Partisan Brigade."

"I beg your pardon. First of all, my comrade scout, we must find a post office and wire home that I've found you safe and sound."

We sent a telegram and also a letter.

Then we went to the station, where our group were staying. My comrades already knew about Ina. We all got acquainted, and Ina received a hearty welcome. Then we prepared breakfast; the feast was laid out on a spread out raincape. The girls insistently offered us jam, candy, and sour milk. I looked serious while moving the sweets away from Ina.

"Scouts are used to dry bread." And I passed a pile of dry bread to her.

"Only when they are reconnoitring behind enemy lines," Ina retorted and piled jam on a piece of bread. We exchanged jokes merrily while having breakfast. Ina was asked to tell about her misadventure. The girls were curious to find out what had happened to her hand.

"Ah, it's just a small burn."

Romanov, Secretary of the Novorzhev Party District Committee, tried to persuade Ina to stay in his group, so that they could cross the front lines together, but she categorically refused. She said she couldn't abandon her comrades-in-arms, who had befriended her, and whom she had accompanied on several combat missions.

"If you only knew what wonderful and brave lads they are!"

Ina told us about her girlfriend Zoya, about a certain Gen'ka, Igor

Glinskiy, and about black Makasha. Listening to her, was saw these boys and girls in our mind's eye as vividly as if they were before us, and we, too, began to like them. About herself she told us drily and briefly:

"Well, I was arrested in Pustoshka. They interrogated me; I was imprisoned and then I ran away. That's all there was to it. And here were our lads, five of them, facing almost an enemy company. Admittedly, the lads were forced to retreat, but surely one would have to be very foolhardy to engage such a force...."

Trucks came to transport the new arrivals to the Tactical HQ. The Brigade was stationed closer to the front lines, preparing for the crossover.

Ina and I went downtown, in search of a truck going our way. We spent about two hours at the frontier command post, but — as if to spite us — not a single truck was going in our direction. A number of officers also waited for a truck. One of them said that there will be a train for Kun'ya that night. We decided to take the train.

At the station we learned that, should there be a train, it would indeed travel at night. We decided to have supper. In a nearby wood we made a campfire and began to boil water in a kettle to make tea. Lying on the grass and drinking tea out of mugs, we quietly conversed. Finally, I persuaded Ina to tell me everything about herself. Her story follows:

Ina crossed the front lines with a group of boys from Lesnikov's detachment. They safely reached the place from which Ina had to proceed by herself. They parted on the best of terms, after deciding on the time and place for their reunion. Ina arrived at the secret address on time, but the man whom she was to meet didn't show up. The success of the onerous task was in jeopardy. Admittedly, she accidentally obtained important information about the enemy. By the way, it proved very useful to the Brigade in its next campaign. But Ina was dissatisfied with herself; she didn't carry out the mission assigned to her by her commander.

Unsuccessfully, Ina attempted to devise various plans of action. In the end, she decided to stay in the area one more day, in order to make inquiries about the individual in question.

She had to find a place to spend the night. She met quite a few female refugees, who entered villages freely to spend the night there; and she, too, decided to sleep over in a village. (By the way, she was hungry — her rations were ending.) It was here that her troubles began.

She met a woman, who appeared sympathetic. She began to question Ina: who was she, where she came from, etc. Ina conscientiously told her "story." The stranger invited her to her home and fed her. And it was only while conversing with the woman in her home that Ina realized her host happened to be the wife of the village elder. The landlady told her that her husband had been expropriated and wronged by the Soviet regime, but see — the Germans were treating them well.

The husband came in, and the couple began to whisper behind a partition. When they came out, they demanded that the guest produce her identification papers. Ina had no choice but to produce them. Her passport issued in the city of Vitebsk had all the necessary endorsements of a German kommandatura. She repeated her story: she had been studying in Velikiye Luki, in a teachers' college, and was on her way to join her parents in Vitebsk; her aunt lived in Pustoshka. In short, she told them a perfectly routine and plausible story.

On hearing her out and carefully examining her passport, the elder was about to return it to her, but his wife advised him to keep it until morning, pending the arrival of a detachment of German troops and police.

Ina pretended she didn't mind, since all along she intended to spend the night in the village. Of course, her heart began to thump. What was she to do? Should she stay here until the morning? Her passport was in order; she was not endangered herself. But the arrival of the German troops would amount to an almost certain death for her comrades. After all, they, suspecting nothing, might well walk straight into German clutches. What was she to do? Should she leave without her passport, she had better stay out of sight of the police. Yet to wait for the lads' return would be tantamount to endangering them, too.

Ina attempted to talk in a calm voice, while mentally examining the alternatives. Finally, she decided to run away. She took out a set of clean underwear out of her kit-bag, called the landlady, and asked to be accompanied to the river so that she could wash herself. The landlady refused to come, but pointed out the best spot for bathing. Ina approached the narrow river, looked around, and without undressing stepped into the water. She quickly crossed the river, up to her neck in water, and came out on the other side. She found herself in a wooded area and kept walking, hoping to meet her comrades halfway. Her dress dried out quite quickly.

Just before dawn, the fugitive stopped for a rest at the forest edge, near the village of Indyka. She slept a bit, but was awakened by the early morning chill. She then chose a high, forested hill as her observation point, because of its unobstructed view. The sun began to warm up; she fell asleep again. About noon she resumed her search for the lads. She heard an exchange of fire nearby; this was probably a punitive detachment combing the woods for the partisans who had attacked a German camp a few days earlier.

Ina wondered along forest paths, looking for footprints, but her search proved in vain. Then she decided to return to the village where she would be more likely to run into the lads. But she feared that here someone might ask her to produce her passport. And, indeed, as soon as she arrived in the village, she ran into a few policemen, who arrested her.

Consequently, she faced the possibility that she might be executed. It was late; she was led into a peasant house. Here she encountered an elder and three policemen, in addition to the landlady. They offered her some milk; she accepted it, but wouldn't talk. Then she lay down on a wooden bench and pretended to be asleep while anxious thoughts — she was becoming more and more terrified — kept going through her mind. "What if the lads had already turned back and returned to the village? They were bound to fall into German clutches. What should I do? If the Germans were to come here, I too am not likely to escape the rope or bullet. I now have no passport. What should I do? How to run away?"

She wanted to go to the outhouse; the landlady accompanied her. The night was dark. After about an hour, she decided to go out again. Apparently, her guards were very sleepy, no one accompanied her this time, and here was the very chance she was waiting for; she got away.

She wandered for about 24 hours, still hoping to meet her party, but she couldn't find them anywhere, so she finally set off for the home base, beyond the front lines. Well, of course, she was hungry, cold, and full of anguish, but she did find her way back. She was ashamed to face her brigade commander, since she hadn't fulfilled her assignment. But when she told him everything, and particularly when she communicated the intelligence she had collected, he even praised her and told her that she had acted correctly.

Ina cheered up and began preparing for another assignment. The lads soon came back, but not all of them; one was killed by his own grenade. It turned out that she had waited and searched for them in vain. They were compelled to come back by a different route; some came alone and some in pairs.

The entire brigade was scheduled to cross over to an enemy-held territory on 28 July, but had to delay its departure until the next day. On 29 July, the Brigade crossed the front lines and kept marching. The partisans advanced for three uneventful days. On the fourth day Ina separated from the Brigade, walking in the direction of the small town of

Alol'. Unexpectedly, she managed to penetrate into the local garrison without encountering any obstacles, and obtained all the requisite intelligence. Then she walked toward the village of Slobodka; inspected certain bridges to determine how they were guarded; and turned toward Pustoshka. She spent the night in a village near the town, entered it in the morning, and by noon fulfilled her assignment. She was — as they say — in seventh heaven: so far, everything turned out well and she scored success after success. It was time to turn back.

As she was leaving the town, Ina saw a long column of trucks loaded with soldiers. While attempting to identify their unit and find out its destination, she was stopped by a policeman who demanded that she produce her passport. She complied. He kept handling the passport for a long time, and then led her to the local Field Kommandatura. Here she was asked a few questions, and after being detained for three hours, was ordered to climb into a truck to be driven under escort to an undisclosed destination.

Ina protested; she made a futile attempt to obtain an explanation for her arrest. In an hour, she was delivered to a captain of gendarmerie in Idritsa. She was led into an office, where she was interrogated through an interpreter, by a grey-haired, fat, and flabby German. Ina again told her fabricated story. The German heard her out, shrugged his shoulders, gave her a crooked smile, and wrote down something. He removed a batch of papers from his desk and put it inside a parcel, then took out a photograph from the parcel, looked at it, wrote something on the reverse side, and put it back inside the parcel. Then he summoned the man responsible for escorting Ina.

Ina asked the interpreter to explain what were the charges against her, and how long would she be detained. He replied that there was a misunderstanding; she'll be taken to Pustoshka and released there. She didn't believe him, and decided to run away at the earliest opportunity.

The escort happened to be a middle-aged German. He brought her to a train station. No sooner they boarded their train when it started moving. In addition to Ina and the German, there were three women and a little boy in the boxcar. Ina attempted to sit down by the door, directly on the floor and with her feet dangling, but the German ordered her to climb on top of the big log lying across the middle of the car, and himself sat down near the door, his rifle across his knees. The train happened to be passing through a forest. "A goodsend!" thought Ina. "How to deceive the escort?" She started a conversation with him. He was overjoyed that the girl spoke

German, and was eager to tell her about his family. As well, he handed her the snapshots of his wife and children. But when Ina, pretending to take a better look at the photographs, got up and walked toward the door, he became frightened and angrily grabbed the shapshots away from her; he then told her to sit down in her old place. "He understood what I had in mind, the German dog!"

On arrival in Pustoshka, the escort brought her to the commandant. Then and there, an interpreter was called, and the interrogation began.

"Where is the detachment? Speak up!"

"What detachment? I don't know anything."

"You lie, you are a partisan."

Ina again told her story. The commandant paced up and down the room in silence. Then he quickly approached his desk, pulled out a drawer, and took out Ina's first "Vitebsk" passport which had been taken away from her some time ago by the village elder.

"Whose passport is it?"

Ina kept silent.

"Speak up!"

His repulsive face reddened. The girl looked him in the eye but said nothing. Next he ran up to her and gave her a blow on the ear with all his strength. And Ina thought: "Never mind. He will get his just deserts!"

"Speak up!" he shouted, choking.

The interpreter mumbled something, but Ina didn't hear what he had said. She stubbornly looked at the officer. Suddenly, he gave out a yelp and hit her in the face a few times. For an instant, Ina lost consciousness. Then she got up. She was dizzy. Her cheek and lip felt wet; she touched them with her hand and saw that the moisture was blood. She placed her hand on the desk and again looked at the commandant. His fingers shaking, he lit up a cigar.

"So you won't talk?"

Again, Ina kept silent.

Then he came closer to her. Suddenly, Ina felt a sharp pain in her right hand resting on the desk.

"I almost screamed," said Ina with clenched teeth, "but the hate I felt toward this vile creature helped me to collect myself and prevented me from breaking down. I bit into my lip. The German swung his arm and threw the cigar into a corner; then he yelled through the door. A man entered and poked me in a shoulder. I understood I was to be taken away."

Ina was taken to a house (this turned out to be the jail), and was pushed into a room with iron bars in the windows. She got up in the middle of the room.... "Well," she thought, "this is the end."

She sat down on the floor, in a corner, and wiped the blood from her face with a kerchief. She was sore all over, but her hand bothered her especially. On it, the ashes of the cigar were still mixed with blood.

She told me: "I felt terrible. And then and there Kashin and our home appeared in my mind's eye. 'What are you all doing now; are you thinking of me?' And I buried myself in the corner and started to cry. Afterwards, I felt better and fell asleep."

She was awakened by a noise; two women and a girl were brought in. They told her that the Germans were searching intensively for girl partisans (by the way, a policeman also said this), so they were grabbing all, even slightly suspicious-looking women. For example, the women were arrested for pushing away a soldier who had been bothering the girl.

Ina cautiously inquired about the location of the jail, the guards, and who were they (the women lived in the town and were well informed about local affairs).

The hand was very sore. Throughout the day she kept applying a wet cloth to it, but the pain persisted and the hand kept swelling up.

In the course of the day the prisoners were given a piece of bread each and a kettle filled with black wish-wash, which was called "coffee." Her sore hand kept Ina awake all night. In the early morning of the third day, a policeman entered the cell and ordered Ina and the other girl, whose name was Dusya, to come out. A fat German wearing a military uniform, stood by the veranda; a pistol hung at his belt. The German led them through the town. When he was asked where he was taking them, he replied in German: "To work!"

The girls were led into the kitchen of an officers' mess. (The fat man turned out to be the chef.) They found two girls already at work there, peeling potatoes and washing dishes. When Ina wanted to take out a basin of dirty water into the yard, the fat man stopped her and let her know that someone else would do it. Ina realized that he was her guard and was responsible for her.

By the time the other girls began to wash dishes after dinner, Ina couldn't do anything: her hand was very swollen and the pain had become unbearable. Ina turned to the chef and asked him in German to take her to a hospital. He agreed, took off his coat and cap, and asked her to follow him. At the hospital she was asked to wait beside the dressing station.

They sat down. The German impatiently sucked on an unlit pipe, and didn't dare to smoke it. Finally, the door opened and Ina was asked to enter the dressing station. The escort told her that he would have a smoke while waiting for her. A nurse examined her hand. She cleaned the wound and applied a dressing, which she attached to the hand with an adhesive. This took no more than five minutes.

When Ina reappeared in the corridor, her escort was nowhere to be found. The door to the yard was open, so she walked out. Her heart was thumping so loud one could almost hear it, and her throat was dry. There was a small pile of firewood by the fence. She slowly walked toward it, and then climbed onto the pile. There was no one behind the fence, so she jumped down onto the street.

She suppressed an urge to run. The sun was behind her, meaning she was walking eastward. When she reached an alley, she mended her pace. She passed a clump of pine-trees and came out onto a highway. Here she turned to the left. She saw a few people walking toward her, and she wondered whether everyone knew about her escape. "Never mind, Inka, never mind, stay calm. A few more minutes and you'll be safely beyond the town; there is a forest on the horizon," she reassured herself. She crossed the second highway, then a marsh, and then a creek. Now she could run! She ran across the water, then across some sedge, and again there was a creek. She wanted to cry from joy. "I am free at last!" The forest kept coming closer and closer, as she walked along the shore of a lake. No, she didn't walk — she flew. Finally, she reached the dear, long-wished for forest and burst into tears. Then she ran for a while, stopped, turned around, shook her fist in the direction of Pustoshka, and began to ran again.

"I kept telling myself," Ina ended her story, "calm down, calm down! Don't rush. Orientate yourself eastward. Well, now, Daddy, that's all there was to it. On the fifth day I was already home. I was lucky. This time, too, all ended well for me."

* * *

On the morning of 4 September, our brigade, included in the 1st Kalinin Partisan Corps consisting of several brigades, set off on a march beyond the front lines. On the night of 10 September we crossed the front lines, without firing a single shot, and advanced deep behind enemy lines.

In this manner, we found ourselves on enemy-occupied territory. We halted, and the Brigade was assigned the first combat mission, involving reconnaissance along the route of advance. The entire formation had to cross the highway and the Nevel' — Polotsk Railroad line. It was decided to carry out raids from the line of march on several stations; our brigade was to attack Zheleznitsa and to destroy the local barracks, an earth-and-timber emplacement, the tracks, and a highway bridge near the station. To attack the barracks, our brigade commander detailed an assault group composed of seven people.

Ina learned that she was not included.

"Why not, Daddy?"

"I don't know, it is up to the commander of the Brigade."

Ina was in tears; the commander had no choice but to give in.

We got ready for the operation. It was a dark September night. The guide, a local peasant, got lost and only just before dawn brought us to the station with great difficulty. We had to hurry. I took Ina and Kolya Dudushkin with me. The three of us crawled right up to the barely discernible barracks. A double log enclosure with earth between the walls surounded the barracks. There were loop-holes all around. We crawled along the enclosure and found an entrance; it was very quiet all around. We stole into the yard; there was not a soul in sight. I sent Kolya to get the remainder of the group. They all made their approach quietly and quickly. We burst into the barracks. There were empty; apparently, the Germans heard the Brigade approach through the forest and retreated to the earth-and-timber emplacement. A green flare went up into the air, which was the signal for an attack. While we were setting fire to the barracks, our second group destroyed the emplacement with mortar bombs and grenades. The Germans opened a furious fire with a heavy machine gun and rifles, but by then we had already carried out our mission, and were slowly retreating into the forest. All around us, explosive bullets made a clicking sound.

I watched Ina; she kept calm, only her face acquired a serious look. Other soldiers conducted themselves in a similar, confident manner.

It was drizzing at daybreak. In an agreed place we assembled for a rest in the village of Malyye Zalogi. Soaked right through but satisfied, we scattered in peasant houses. In the evening Ina and several men set off to reconnoitre our further route of advance.

This was the beginning of our partisan existence.

By 22 September we reached the area of Sherstovo — Bezzubenki — Yerastovka. Ina took part in several dangerous reconnoitring ventures.

There were many remarkable encounters. I particularly remember one of them, on a hill near the farmstead called Alekseyevka.

Ina lay behind a sandy hillock. I joined her and lay down beside her. It was a bright, sunny, and warm day. A field, from which came the sound of a fierce exchange of fire, was clearly visible. German troops stubbornly advanced toward us.

We were thirsty, so we sent one scout beyond the farmstead to get some water. He hadn't come back when a woman carrying a pail emerged from behind a clump of bushes. She kept climbing our hill, frequently stopping to rest. Ina rushed toward her.

"Grandmother, where are you going?"

"To you, my children. Here is some milk for you, be my guests."

"What came over you, grandmother! It is dangerous here."

"Never mind, my child, I am not afraid. Here have some milk." The old woman passed the pail to Ina. "It is warm, my child. I've just milked the cow. I've a little cow right here, in the forest."

To protect her from stray bullets, we seated the old lady behind a thick pine-tree.

We drank the milk and thanked the kind woman. She kept asking Ina about her family, and when she learned that I was her father, tears stood in her eyes.

"My children, so you came here through the front lines. Well, how is it possible? And I thought you were local people. And you, my little daughter, why did you come? You should leave the fighting to the men. You must find it very hard. It's not a woman's business. It's scary."

"What came over you, grandmother! See there, you too were not afraid to come here."

"I am old; I'll soon die anyway, but your life, my little daughter, is still ahead of you; you mustn't throw it away."

"That's it, I do value life, that's why I came here. After we have chased the Germans away, we'll live gloriously.... Thank you, grandmother, for the milk."

The woman got up and wiped away her tears with a corner of her kerchief. Ina gave her a hug and helped her to come down the slope. And then we followed the woman with our eyes for a long time as she slowly walked away in the direction of the farmstead.

Meanwhile, the exchange of fire ceased. A messenger came from the commander. He informed us that the enemy had retreated after sustaining heavy losses in both dead and wounded.

At night we reconnoitred the route toward Idritsa, while Ina rested. In the morning of the following day, a few carts loaded with wounded partisans went past us. Suddenly, someone called out:

"Aleksandr Pavlovich!"

I approached the cart.

"Gennadiy, what has happened to you?"

"Well, as you can see, I got hit in the leg."

"Is it a serious wound?"

"Not too bad, but I am being sent across the front lines."

I called Ina. She escorted our fellow-countryman to the village of Sherstovo, where a hospital was located.

In two hours Ina came back; she was crying.

"I can't stand seeing people suffer! Gennadiy is in a terrible pain. He fears that they might amputate his leg. I feel so sorry for him and his comrades! Tomorrow morning they will be transported across the front lines.... What if they are caught by the Germans? The beasts are not likely to spare them."

I tried to calm her down, and advised her to write a letter home, to be taken across the front lines with the wounded. Ina obediently applied herself to this task.

Our brigade advanced all night. We marched along the highway to Rossony [in Belorussia]. The road was blocked in many places; there were many blown up bridges. In daytime we rested in villages. German garrisons were all around, but the enemy hesitated to attack us. Three days passed in this manner.

Then we approached the Velikiye Luki — Sebezh Railroad. Ina had just returned from reconnoitring. It was two in the morning; we decided to rest. The crossing was scheduled for the following night.

I remember that morning so well. It was quiet and cool. The area was dry and had a high elevation; it was overgrown with thick moss. All around us the pines were whispering.

We found a depression and pitched a tent.

"It feels like lying on a feather bed!" said Ina.

She looked pensively at the stars.

"At home Mom and Reginka are now fast asleep," speculated Ina. "And we are so far apart! Who would have thought, Daddy, that things would turn out this way! You and I fighting together.... How fast everything has changed! It seems to me it was only yesterday when I was cramming my lessons and dreamed about attending the Aviation Institute, and now all one wishes for is a warm blanket.... Truly, Daddy," she said, laughing, "is a warm blanket the only thing that we are now missing to be perfectly happy?"

We lay like this talking quietly. It was getting cold. I got up and quickly took a large handful of dry moss, which I placed on top of the tent.

"Here is a warm blanket for you."

We fell asleep.

The next day we crossed the tracks and on the following day we arrived in the village of Mayuzino. We found out that a dairy was located about 8 kilometres from the village, and a detachment of police was stationed in the building of the local small rural district administration. The peasant population of the area had been ordered to bring milk to the dairy; moreover, the Germans had gone on rampage in neighboring villages, looting peasant houses and taking eggs and lard away from them.

A small scouting party was assigned the task of burning down the dairy.

Ina crawled alongside me. At dawn our group surrounded the barracks of the dairy security force.

"Fire!"

Several random shots rang out in reply. We burst into the barracks.

One of those caught there cried pitifully: "Don't shoot, I am one of your people, a partisan."

Ina quickly ran up to him and grabbed the rifle out of his hand. Meanwhile, our men swiftly picked up the weapons, equipment, and ammunition abandoned by the guards. An armful of straw was blazing up. The fire spread quickly. And there was Ina — against the background of the burning barracks — wearing a padded jacket and armed with a carbine. In front of her, the lanky fellow, wearing a helmet, was mumbling pitifully and inarticulately. The girl looked to one side — and there was so much contempt and squeamishness in her eyes!

The dairy was burning. We ran toward the district administration. Ina approached me: "Comrade Deputy Brigade Commander! Give me an order to pass the prisoner to one of your men."

I called one man and ordered him to escort the policeman to the assembly hall.

"You know," Ina whispered to me, "I can't look at him, he makes me want to throw up: I find him so abominable, so disgusting! I want to spit into his 'pagan' mug. How could he work for the Germans? What an accursed coward!"

Soon the local government building was taken care of, too. We retreated to our camp in the forest.

In the morning our reconnaissance party reported that the Germans were preparing an expedition against us. I gathered a few scouts and went to set up an ambush at a crossroads. The men took up positions on a hill in a clump of bushes. Behind us was a small farmstead; a single apple-tree grew in the orchard. At the top of the tree, among the yellowing leaves, by the light of the sun which was peaking through, I saw a miraculously preserved apple. I had a mischievious urge: I crawled down from the hill and knocked the apple off with a stick. I went back and handed the apple to Ina.

"My darling Daddy, where did you get it?" she exclaimed. "Well, if it isn't 'Antonovka'!" She took out a knife, cut the apple in half, and handed one half to me. I refused. "No, no, take it," she said. "We must share it. How long is it since I had an apple? Do you remember how abundant fruit was in the Caucasus? It was so long ago! Do you remember the sea? So calm, benign, particularly in the evenings, and constantly whispering.... And do you remember how you and I caught a turtle in the mountains and how Reginka carried it in her arms?"

"I remember, I remember it all. I even remember how you didn't get along with the Young Pioneer [junior branch of the Komsomol] leader and was capricious," I say with a smile.

"But, Daddy, I was so foolish then...."

A German machine gun kept firing to the right of our location; rifle shots rang out in reply. One of the local partisans determined that the exchange of fire took place by the river crossing.

We got up and took a shortcut through the forest, advancing quickly toward the crossing on the Velikaya River. The rate of fire decreased. We walked along a deep ravine; then we crawled upward to the summit. Next we went to ground.

"There are Germans to the right of us, in the bushes," whispered Ina.

I raised my binoculars and clearly distinguished the silhouettes in grey-green uniforms on the opposite shore, about 200 metres away. Apparently, the Germans were not numerous. They were "feeling" the crossing; from the nearest bushes a German machine gun fired in short bursts. We fixed its position. I ordered our group to open fire with machine guns and rifles. Kolya Vinogradov set up his machine gun beside me. A long burst followed. Ina, taking a careful aim, fired her carbine systematically. German explosive bullets clicked overhead.

Vinogradov changed his position. I saw how the green silhouettes hid behind the bushes. The bullet whistling and explosions overhead stopped; the enemy began to retreat.

After a while, two partisans and Ina crossed the river. In about an hour, the scouts returned with a German field service cap, mess-tin, and spoon. They reported that, judging by the footprints, there were twenty-five to thirty Germans with one machine gun at the crossing place. They had retreated toward Idritsa.

In the afternoon, Ina and I went reconnoitring on horseback; a local partisan guided us. We soon managed to determine that the Germans were concentrating their forces. We decided to wait until it got dark, since it would have been dangerous to continue reconnoitring in broad daylight.

We took up our positions on a small, forested hill. The horses, hobbling, grazed in the ravine. It was a fall evening. The sun gilded the tips of the pine-trees; birch-trees and aspens stood in their fall attire. The rustle of the forest was barely audible. Before us was a calm lake.

"Take a look Daddy, how nice it is all around. What a marvellous country! What a beautiful lake, and what pine-trees: a place to enjoy, not fight." I looked at my daughter. A stubborn lock of hair escaped from under her kerchief; a golden little tress fell on her shoulder.

"Daddy, after the war has ended, a resort ought to be built here, without fail. People should come here to rest, enjoy the marvellous view, breathe the pure air, and bathe in the lake. They would be free to take walks, whether in daytime or nighttime, without having to hide as we must do now. A beautiful building should be constructed over there," she pointed with her hand, "with a wide stairway leading down. The swimming pool should be built here, and the flat ground would be suitable for flower beds.... OK?"

"We'll come here to rest and reminisce about our partisan life," I joined in, involuntarily affected by my daughter's mood. "We'll go canoeing, just as we did on the Black Sea."

"And Mom will sit over there, by the pine-trees, on a bench, and she'll admonish us: 'Be careful or else you'll drown'!" interjected Ina. "Mom! What is she doing at this very moment? If only she could see us now." Ina turned her head toward the setting sun. "Daddy, Daddy, look, what a wonderful view!"

Later on that night, we went on a mission: we were assigned the demolition of two big bridges on the Slobodka — Kholyuny Highway. It was drizzling and you couldn't see a thing. We walked in a single file holding hands. The rain intensified and our clothing gradually became soaked. It was cold. In a tiny village located in the forest we picked up two sheaves of straw each. Then we walked to the highway; German motor vehicles rarely passed here. Five of our scouts, who had prepared their hand grenades, crawled toward the bridge. Ina crawled ahead of me. The silhouette of the bridge loomed ahead of us. Ina and one of the young lads quietly got up and walked along the Highway. Tension mounted as we were waiting. Then we heard a whisper from above:

"There is no guard, Daddy."

I refused to believe this: only the day before the bridge was guarded. I got up and walked onto the bridge. It was deserted. In ten minutes the men brought the straw. The bridge burned, but not too well: the wet logs of the flooring didn't catch fire. Then we placed balls of Thermit on the bridge, and at once a bright flame shot up. Just then, a skirmish began to the left of us, meaning that our second group had attacked the passing enemy motor vehicles. We destroyed the second bridge, too.

Toward daybreak it got colder, even though the rain had stopped. We retreated into the forest (clothing dried on our bodies). Ina approached me and asked: "Have you got a piece of bread?"

A piece of dry bread turned up in my map case. I gave it to her.

During the next day we rested for several hours in a village. Then we continued marching. On the way, Ina was reconnoitring. We destroyed several rural district administration buildings along our way. Now and then the scouts exchanged fire with punitive detachments. Local young people joined our ranks; two new detachments were formed. There was not enough weapons.

Observing my daughter, I could tell that she was satisfied with herself, realizing that she was a needed, useful person. I was proud of her; I saw how respected she was by her comrades, and how she was appreciated by her superiors. I must admit that in my heart of hearts I often feared for her safety. During moments of danger, I tried to be close to her; I felt that she, too, looked out for me and tried to stay near me.

The HQ of the partisan brigade rewarded Ina for her exploits by granting her leave to go home on a visit. She went to her hometown of Kashin.

Some weeks later, a sentry came into the HQ and reported that the man in charge of the reconnaissance party of our No. 2 detachment, nicknamed Misha Petrov, had arrived and had asked permission to see me. Misha entered (his real name was Vsevolod Ivanovich Gorbach).

"Aleksandr Pavlovich, I've brought you a gift!"

"What kind of a gift?"

"Make a guess," smiled Misha. "A very precious gift. Expected here in a half hour."

And in fact, within a half hour, several sleds drove up to the building; the door opened and in rushed Ina. She threw herself on my neck; hugged and kissed me. She brought me greetings from many people and a lot of letters from home, as well as some tobacco, which she had managed to carry across the front lines. At that time tobacco was a great rarity for us. We smoked a home-grown kind, which happened to be very nasty.

By evening the weather got worse, and the planes didn't come. I was free to talk at length with Ina about the news from the "Mainland." She told me about all kinds of things, without taking a break, and most of all about Mom and Rena, with whom she had managed to spend a whole month. We talked all night until dawn.

On 5 May 1943 Ina became seriously ill, having come down with tonsillitis and subsequently with ulcerous stomatitis. We lived in a forest, where nights were very cold. We couldn't keep the sick with us under such conditions, and we placed them in forest farmsteads. In one or two days they had to be moved to new places, now by a boat on the Velikaya River and now by a partisan cart. Ina's illness took a very serious turn, and there was not a single medical worker in the detachment. We treated her with home remedies, but when her entire mouth cavity became covered with ulcers, I decided to bring, at the very least, a doctor's assistant from the district hospital. This was not an easy task, as it had to be done without alerting the enemy.

I rode to the hospital at night, accompanied by one scout. After awakening the medic, I persuaded him to come to an agreed place, in order to examine Ina. The examination took place the next day, but the medic had only lunar caustic at his disposal, which he used to cauterize the ulcers in Ina's mouth. How she must have suffered, the poor girl! But she stoically withstood everything. I continued the treatment myself. After two or three cauterizations Ina began to recover. Nevertheless, she was still very weak.

Around this time we were getting ready to raid an enemy garrison in the village of Guzhovo of Idritsa District.

We were scheduled to attack the garrison on 26 May. I summoned the detachment. We began crossing the river about an hour later. Suddenly, I saw Ina amongst us.

"What are you doing here? You'll end up by killing yourself. After all, you can barely walk," I whispered to her.

"Daddy, darling, what else is there for me to do but join you?" It was useless to argue with her.

Having burst into the village, we captured the company commander and thirty soldiers, without firing a single shot. We began to transport the prisoners and weapons across the river. Suddenly, an enemy section — that knew nothing about the raid — returned to the village from reconnoitring. None of my men happened to be handy then, and we had to act quickly.

I summoned Ina and briefly described the situation to her. We advanced toward the soldiers; I was counting on taking them by surprise. As we approached them, I saw, in the pre-dawn mist, their machine-gunner carrying his weapon on his shoulder. We came right up to them, and in a loud voice I ordered them to lay down their arms. A moment of confusion ensued. Ina began to grab the rifles away from the soldiers. Soon the machine gun was in our possession too. Arriving in time, our partisans surrounded the Germans and quickly finished disarming them.

It all transpired so quickly that nobody of the prisoners had the time to realize what was really happening. Later on they admitted that it was only when they reached the far shore of the Velikaya River that they noticed the stars on the caps of our men in the daylight and understood who had captured them. And two days later, during an interrogation, a captive platoon commander voiced his surprise at the resoluteness of the girl who had taken part in the disarming of his soldiers.

Ina was herself pleased with the results of this action; the booty was significant: a mortar, two machine guns, thirty rifles, mines, cartridges, food, horses, and carts.

I'll never forget how, subsequently, while we were resting, Ina treated me to *gogol'-mogol'* she had made from captured eggs and sugar.[1]

"We can well afford the delicacy today!"

That day I presented her with my tiny pistol which she so wanted to have.

I was often struck by her ability to combine adult traits, such as seriousness, with purely childish habits, and at times I was amazed by her spontaneity. On a number of occasions, while listening to her conversations with her comrades-in-arms, I overheard her talking about the books she had read, Moscow, art, the situation at the front, and then and there she would suddenly burst out laughing, merry, noisy, and chattering like

a child. She knew how to appeal to both adult and child and was respected by both. In every village she had friends among children and old people
especially. Often, in passing though a village with Ina, you could hear
people calling to her:

"Ina, Inochka, come to see us!"

"Ina, come and eat with us!"

"Will you have some milk or berries?"

And Ina found time to call on everyone. Now she went to talk with a
woman or an old man; now she stroked a child, letting him ride her horse;
now she dropped for a minute to pass the latest news heard on the radio;
and now she supplied a sick man with a medication. At every place we
stopped, she very quickly made friends. The housewives kept spoiling her,
proffering their tastiest dishes, providing the most comfortable accom-
modation, and doing all kinds of favours for her.

She taught herself to ride a horse very quickly and competently. No
matter how tired, hungry or cold she might be, she always looked after her
animal first. Though she loved to sleep, she never failed to get up several
times during the night to inspect the horse, and to give it some more
fodder.

Dressed in men's blue overalls, she rode a small, very lively white
horse. I often admired her when she adroitly sat in the saddle, eyes
sparkling and hair flying. She would approach me, then suddenly rein her
horse, and report on the results of her reconnoitring.

And here is a picture which stayed in my mind's eye, too. Thick
shrubs near a path running by the edge of a forest. About 500 metres from
the path you could see a highway, along which an enemy column was
marching. A girl (Ina), wearing blue overalls, on a white horse and standing
in her stirrups, was looking attentively at the highway, her lips moving and
hand squeezing a submachine gun. Beside her was a young boy (Vadim
Nikonenok), on a black horse; he was carefully examining the road leading
into the forest. The observation post had been very well chosen: the
highway was clearly visible, and the observers were concealed by the thick
shrubs. So, half an hour later, Ina was already in a position to report on
the enemy's numerical strength and armament.

Fidgety and impatient, she nevertheless could remain motionless for
hours while reconnoitring, without missing a single detail, however minor.

We took part in action after action throughout June. Ina, going almost
without rest, was either reconnoitring or participated in railroad or highway
sabotage actions. Invariably, she would return to the detachment satisfied

with the results. She kept telling me: "Daddy, I've become convinced that we are needed here. We've caused so much trouble, so far, to the Germans! How nervous they are, how they rush about in search of the partisans! Partisans derail trains, blow up motor vehicles, and set fire to bridges every day. Isn't this enough?"

In July 1943 a small group of saboteurs, including Ina, blew up a German troop train between Idritsa and the siding of Yalovka. It proved impossible for them to check the results immediately after the explosion, even though they were anxious to know what had been accomplished. And so in two days the group set off for the site of the crash. After taking a look and convincing themselves that the results were fairly good — six railway cars were still lying derailed (the locomotive had already been raised by the Germans) — the saboteurs set off for home.

While crossing the highway, they decided to set up an ambush. The place was not really suitable for this, but they could not resist the temptation. They took up positions in the ditch, beside the highway. Shortly afterwards, a motorcycle appeared on the highway. "Most likely, an officer," the scouts decided. "A good prey." When the motorcycle came alongside them, they opened fire. It stopped. Then the entire group rushed onto the highway. In that moment, a few trucks, loaded with soldiers, came from beyond a bend in the highway; the soldiers opened fire at the partisans.

The position of the partisans became desperate: there were five of them facing fifty enemy soldiers armed with machine guns. Moreover, the escaping partisans had to make their way through an open terrain. The soldiers, noting that the partisans were few, jumped out of their trucks. After half-enveloping the group, they kept firing on the move.

Ina ran last, firing back short submachine-gun bursts. An explosive bullet ripped out a piece of fabric from her jacket. An officer followed her, firing a pistol; he prompted her to surrender. Only 10 metres remained between them; at any moment his bullet could have hit her. She had almost reached the forest, but the enemy was drawing even nearer. When the officer was on the point of grabbing her, Ina let go a burst over her shoulder. In that moment, a fellow-partisan who had managed to reach the forest opened fire. The Germans immediately stopped and went to ground. This gave Ina sufficient time to disappear among the trees. Coincidentally, a few bursts from behind the trees forced the Germans to stop their pursuit.

After covering a short distance inside the forest, Ina's fellow partisans looked around. The side of Ina's jacket and a half of its sleeve were torn out, the stock of her submachine gun was pierced, but she herself was lucky to escape without a single scratch.

"Well, how did you like the motorcycle? Did you take the officer and his map case?" the scouts joked afterwards.

On this occasion Ina was saved by a sheer miracle. As she told me later: "I no longer had any hopes of escaping; I expected a bullet in my back at any moment. Yet I couldn't stop, because then the soldiers would have surely surrounded me. Of course, I didn't want to die, but I held my submachine gun in a way that would enable me to fire at myself should the officer grab me, or I were about to fall down.... What really mattered was that the submachine gun was intact. Take a look: now it can be easily distinguished; it is well-marked!" And she stroked her submachine gun, admiring it.

Ina spent the entire month of July in a flanking detachment, carrying out various missions every day. At the beginning of August she rejoined me, in order to fly out into the rear area and go back to school, under orders from her superiors. One day, the commander of the Brigade and I were sitting at the HQ, planning operational missions. The problem was how to approach the railway track along which the guard had been doubled of late by the enemy. The reconnaissance parties of our brigade, as well as other brigades, reported that it has become very difficult to cross the track.

Suddenly, a rider came up to the house. Looking out of the window, I saw Ina getting off her horse. I told the commander:

"Look, Nikolay Vasil'yevich! Ina has just come from the railway, and on horseback at that; hence, the devil is not as black as he Is painted."

Ina entered. "Comrade Brigade Commander, partisan Konstantinova reporting." We were eager to question her.

"Yes, the Germans have doubled their guard along the track, but it is possible to approach it and cross it. I went out there with a group of saboteurs from the 3rd Brigade. They warned me that one couldn't cross it on horseback, and advised me to leave the horse in the detachment. But how could I leave my Mashka behind? I believed that I could cross the railway. We couldn't do it the first night; when we were approaching the track, the Germans discovered us, so we tried to cross it in a more remote place. Again we had to turn back, and spent the day in the forest. I argued with the lads, trying to convince them that the Germans tend to wait for us in a forested, out-of-the-way places, but are absent at open crossings. All the same, they decided to cross in places to which they were accustomed.

"As soon as it got dark, we started out. We reached the road leading to one level crossing. Here I said good-bye to my companions, wishing them success. I waited for about an hour, and then I carefully took Mashka's rein, and approached the track. It was quiet; the Germans fired infrequently, as usual, but this suited me just fine, meaning that all was well along the track. I climbed into the saddle and galloped across; literally, in half a minute I came out onto the other side of the roadbed. When I was galloping across the highway without slowing down, I heard yelling behind me and, later on, some shots as well. But by then I had already entered the forest, and the bullets that were exploding behind me were too high. This is how I got through. May I attend to my horse, Comrade Brigade Commander?"

Nikolay Vasil'yevich shook his head and said: "What a smart girl you are!"

He instructed his orderly to take away Ina's horse, but she wanted to do it herself. So we had to let her go. In half an hour, during dinner, she described the situation in the area of her detachment and her plans for the nearest future.

Ina rode out to the airfield several times, but our aircraft weren't flying at that time. She went reconnoitring and took part in the "rail war" on the Novosokol'niki — Idritsa line.

On 28 September, a large punitive detachment equipped with three artillery pieces, several battalion mortars, and a large number of heavy machine guns attacked the positions of our brigade. The shells exploded around us, but our partisans behaved very valiantly. I observed Ina; her face revealed no consternation or fear, and she was completely calm. With her submachine gun at the ready, she carefully watched the dell before us, and from time to time looked back into the forest where our horses were tied up.

The next day Ina told me, among other things, about the behaviour of my horse, which would lie down as soon as artillery fire started.

"So you see," I replied, "that even a horse understands that it makes no sense to take unnecessary risks, while many of our young people, including yourself, even flaunt the fact that they don't go to ground and take cover."

Ina pretended to agree with me, yet attempted to convince me that recklessness could be justifed at times, particularly when it was necessary to embolden one's fellow soldiers.

On one occasion our detachment was engaged in a skirmish with a punitive expedition in the vicinity of the village of Kurilovo in Idritsa District. We pinpointed the location of the enemy, and I climbed a hillock overgrown with tall pine-trees. Ina followed me very closely to the summit. She was anxious to spot the enemy herself, so she wanted to get up on her tiptoes, in order to have a better view; I forbade her to do it. We were on the lookout for some time. Then I noticed several enemy soldiers about 400 metres from us, and I told Ina, who was lying behind me, about this. She wanted to see for herself, so she got up and stood beside a pine-tree. In about a minute explosive bullets began to click all around us, and a fragment scratched my finger. We had to abandon our lookout.

Coming down the hill, I jokingly blamed her for provoking "this spilling of my blood." At first she tried to argue that it happened accidentally. In a few days, while we were back in this area, she checked the visibility of the hillock from the place previously occupied by the Germans. That evening, when Ina returned, she honestly admitted to me that she had been in the wrong.

As a general rule it was Ina's characteristic trait to be honest about her mistakes. I remember how, still before the war, Ina got into an argument with her mother, and went out after slamming the front door. Five minutes passed; Ina returned and with tears in her eyes begged her mother's forgiveness, admitting that she had been in the wrong; and she didn't leave the house until she was convinced that her mother had forgiven her.

Over and over again, Ina spared no effort in trying to prove that she was in the right and in defending herself, but as soon as she realized she was mistaken, she mustered the courage to admit it.

Toward the end of September, a few messengers came to us from an adjacent detachment to obtain explosives. Ina asked permission to accompany them, so she could pick up the warm clothing she had left behind in that detachment. At first I didn't want to let her go, but she insisted and I hadn't the heart to refuse her. She promised to return in nine to twelve days. On 5 October we parted in the village of Gorbachevo of Rossony District, and she proceeded to the northern part of Idritsa District, to the detachment.

I accompanied her beyond the village. Ina walked, holding onto my stirrup, and all along begged me not to worry about her. We said good-bye to each other. I kept following Ina with my eyes for a long time, and she kept turning around and waving to me. It was with this gesture that she disappeared in the forest, beyond the turn of the road. That's how I saw my Inochka for the last time.

It proved impossible for her to come back. In our sector the offensive of the Red Army created new front lines which would separate us for ever. Moreover, on 12 November I was wounded and evacuated to a hospital, while Ina stayed behind in her detachment.[2]

* * *

My knowledge about the final period of Ina's life is derived solely from what I had been told by her comrades and friends.

In the winter of 1944 our partisans experienced very hard times. The front lines moved away to the west; it became "crowded" behind enemy lines. Ina's detachment operated in areas adjacent to the front lines, while the enemy either burned down the settlements in the detachment's operating area or occupied them with large garrisons. It proved necessary to seek cover in the woods. Partisan forest camps were subjected to frequent attacks by large enemy forces and the partisans were often compelled to move from place to place. They had to put up with hastily made dugouts, and not infrequently lived in the open, too.

Ina's girlfriends told me that she was never downcast, and tried to keep up her comrades' spirits in all kinds of ways. She often initiated conversations about the future. She would say: "Never mind, girls, it won't be long before our troops start pressing the Germans; we'll help them from the rear, and then we'll have good times. We'll return to Moscow; we'll go to theatres, movies, and museums."

And Ina would then describe Moscow, its theatres, and the Tret'yakov Gallery. She made remarkable plans; her confidence, good spirits, and gayety were infectious. Entire scenes have been generated before my mind's eye, on the basis of her comrades' stories. There is Ina in a yellow sheepskin coat and hat sitting on a stump. She is drawing something on the snow with a stick, while conversing with Vadik[3] Nikonenok. In her spare time she spent hours with him, engrossed in a spirited discussion.

"Well, what are you two conversing about, Ina?" asked the girls. "Aren't you bored talking to such a young boy?"

"But he is so interesting, so precocious! He has so many questions to ask, and displays such a thirst for knowledge! So I am explaining various things to him. He is so interesting to talk to!"

Sometimes Ina rode to Vadik's native village, and visited his family.

Vadik's tiny, two-year-old sister Verochka reacted to Ina's visits with enthusiasm, babbling in a child's tongue. Now Ina would place her in the saddle to give her a ride, and now she would present some toy to her. The child became very attached to Ina. To this day she has kept as a souvenir a red button which Ina had given her so long ago.

The Germans pursued the detachment relentlessly; skirmishes, exchanges of fire occurred daily. The partisans' ammunition was almost exhausted; yet there were no airstrips to receive supply aircraft. Short of cartridges, the partisans nevertheless had to fight, had to attack.

Here is a scenario in my mind's eye: to the left of a crossroads in a thick pine forest, a girl in a sheepskin coat (Ina), armed with a submachine gun, and a boy (Vadik), armed with a rifle, were observing the road. A detachment of German troops was advancing along a road. The girl and the boy carefully examined and counted the enemy men and equipment. The column passed; it was followed by a cart loaded with ammunition. The driver had barely stopped at the crossroads, not knowing where to go, when the girl with a submachine gun came out of the forest and very eloquently indicated the "right" direction. The driver turned the horse around. And in two hours Ina's detachment was rejoicing, for she had delivered to them a cart loaded with ammunition.

Weeks passed, difficult weeks, full of hardship and danger; spring was approaching. The first few warm days cheered up the partisans; soon the snow would melt, the new leaves would come out, and it would be easier to fight the enemy and to hide. Ina with her girlfriend Dusya Skovoroda went on a mission, walking in the direction of the front lines. By nighttime they reached a forest dugout. After consulting with comrades in it, they devised a plan for future actions; then they fell asleep. Just before dawn, the sentry woke them up to tell them that their dugout was surrounded by a detachment of German soldiers.

Ina jumped out of the dugout; she understood that it would be impossible for all of them to escape. The enemy had already half-enveloped their camp. It made no sense for all of them to return fire either, since the opposing forces were so unequal. Somebody had to cover the retreat, so that at least a few could be saved. Dropping on one knee, Ina began to fire her submachine gun; the shots made a clicking sound and the bullets whistled. Wearing a grey turtleneck sweater and a hat with a red ribbon, a small pistol and a submachine gun disk at her belt, Ina kept firing short bursts at the grey-green silhouettes flashing between trees and bushes. Squealing bullets flew all around her, making a smacking sound on the frozen, March snow crust, cutting off branches from the trees and bushes. Her accurate burst stopped the enemy for only about a minute, but the time proved sufficient for Ina's comrades to hide in the forest thicket.

The ring around Ina was becoming smaller and smaller....

The next night, Ina's comrades came back. They picked up the lifeless body of the girl and buried her on a sandy hill under whispering pines.[4] One one pine, the partisans cut out a single word: "INA."

In 1949, Ina's remains were transferred to a cemetery in her home town of Kashin.[5]

NOTES

1.   A simple and tasty snack produced by whipping raw egg yolks with sugar.

2.   In light of the above, I placed Ina's two undated letters which in the original text follow her letter dated 16 December 1943 ahead of the latter. See Note 5 to Partisan: 1943-1944.

3.   Diminutive of "Vadim."

4.   In the vicinity of Pustoshka. See Minayeva, *et al.*, eds., *Srazhalas'*, p. 12.

5.   On 18 November 1949 Ina was posthumously awarded the "Partisan of Patriotic War" Medal, II Class. See Minayeva, *et al.*, eds., *loc. cit.*

FOR THE SAKE OF LIFE ON EARTH

G. Astaf'yev and D. Petrov

A bullet found her and her life was ended, cut short by a piece of lead in a nickel casing. Yet she still lives and will live forever; in our contemporaries, our children, and our children's children.

Ina Konstantinova attended Secondary School No. 1 in Kashin. Hence, the Young Pioneer[1] squad of the School was named after her; and the best performing young Pioneer detachment assumes the right to bear her name too. When the first school bell rings, perfectly ordinary boys and girls sit down behind their desks. And the teacher, before starting the lesson, asks a perfectly ordinary question of the duty pupil: "Who is absent today?"

He or she replies: "Ina Konstantinova is absent. The brave partisan died in combat, resisting the Nazi invaders.... Everyone else is present."

Everyone else is present. Only she is absent. But everything is as before. The very same rustling of pages in the classroom. The very same sun outside the windows. The very same sky. And just as it happened many years ago, short-haired and mop-like backs of heads stick out above the desks. She was like that, too.

An inscription on one of the schoolroom doors reads: "Ina studied here." In the classroom, the second desk from the window bears another inscription: "Ina sat behind this desk." In a display case on the wall in the corridor, there are ordinary amateur snapshots of Ina, an ordinary young girl: one of Ina in the classroom, another one of Ina attending an amateur concert, and still another of Ina walking in the woods. Little girls examine the display case, noting that she was no different from them. And yet she died a hero's death.

How did she manage to do it? They know how; they have read Ina's diary, a remarkable historical document. They drop into the School's Museum. They write naive, amateurish letters to war veterans. They are active in the "Patriot" Club and, on the nights of 22 February and 8 May [Red Army Day and V-Day respectively] each year they carry out Operation "Red Star."

On these nights, and on the eve of 7 November [an anniversary of the October Revolution] and May Day, red stars appear on the doors of houses and apartments occupied by war veterans.[2] And under each of

109

these stars there is a short statement highlighting the soldier's career, so that others might learn about him.

The pupils of the school which Ina had attended collect photographs, documents, and letters. They have enough to fill out many large rooms of a sizeable museum. So far their exhibits are housed in one room only. There are dozens of museum guides among senior students. They know a lot, quite a lot about Ina. They tell everything about her to the visitors of the Museum. And in the process they, themselves, constantly learn more about her. They keep gaining new insights from their simple photographs and documents.

Here is a small piece of paper yellowed by time; it reads as follows:

CERTIFICATE

"This is to certify that I.A. Konstantinova trained in a volunteer aid detachment set up by the Kashin District Committee of the Red Cross, Russian Republic Branch. Upon graduation, her performance was rated 'excellent' overall. Dated 25 July 1941."

As mentioned, in Kashin the Young Pioneer squad and detachments of Secondary School No. 1 have been named after Ina. As well, in a number of Young Pioneer detachments her name had been written down in classroom logbooks. Remembering Ina is a way of expressing the continuity between the succeeding generations and the unbreakable bond between them.

The Museum in her school is visited by many people, both children and adults, local inhabitants and tourists alike. They sign their names and comment in the guest book. One such comment, signed by Young Pioneers of Grade 4A, Secondary School, Settlement of Vasil'yevskiy Mokh, Kalinin District, reads: "We are very impressed by the Museum at Kashin Secondary School No. 1. We hope to have our detachment named after Ina Konstantinova. Now that we have visited your Museum, we will do our utmost to prove worthy of this great honour."

In her home town, one street and a square now bear Ina's name. She is buried in a simple grave. On the marble headstone, there is an inscription in gold letters:

Partisan
KONSTANTINOVA
Inessa Aleksandrovna

$$19\frac{30}{VII}24 - 19\frac{4}{III}44$$

Here, too, is the memorable phrase excerpted from a letter to her mother, dated 7 November 1942:

"And I am having a wonderful youth...."

On the other side, another excerpt reads: "To be alive and to live.... Can there be anything greater, anything more wonderful!"

There are flowers and wreaths on the grave at all times. A simple red star has been affixed to the grave by a child's hand, and the inscription below the star, signed "Young Pioneers and Komsomols, Secondary School No. 1 in Kashin," reads as follows: "Stop Comrade! Bare your head and bend your knees! Before you is the grave of Ina Konstantinova, a worthy daughter of her Homeland, who sacrificed her life, her most prized possession, during the war against the Nazis. Dear Ina: your life will always serve as an inspiration to us."

Many people make special trips to Kashin, in order to learn more about Ina, to see her home town, and to walk along its quiet streets in the knowledge that "She walked here too." The influx of visitors has increased after the publication of the original version of the *Girl from Kashin*. Visitors are still coming not only from Kalinin Region, and from adjacent regions, but even from as far as the Far East, Siberia, and the Urals. For instance, a university student in Leningrad put away a ruble at a time from her meagre scholarship so she could visit Ina's home town.

In Kashin, the modest wooden house in which Ina had lived still stands at 4 High Soviet Street. It is now occupied by her sister, Regina Aleksandrovna. Ina's room has been preserved in its original state. There is a metal bed covered with a white bedspread. In the corner between the bed and the window stands a small mahogany night table with three drawers. A mahogany chair has been placed beside Ina's desk, at which she did her homework. Her diary was kept in the left drawer of this desk.

A bookcase hangs over the desk, with two rows of her books in it: collections of Mayakovskiy's poetry, textbooks, and more poems. A portrait of Mayakovskiy hangs on the wall.

Fig. 8. The pine-tree under which Ina was buried

Fig. 9. The headstone on Ina's grave in Kashin

The desk of Ina's father, Aleksandr Pavlovich, stands here too. On it there are several small bundles of letters tied with a string. Among them are letters addressed to Ina's parents written by total strangers who read the original version of *The Girl from Kashin*.

There are letters from friends of the family as well. But the majority of letters are from schoolchildren, those who are members of Young Pioneer squads named after Ina, or those who are anxious that their squads and detachments qualify for this honour.

There are others things beside letters. The young Pioneers of Junior Secondary School No. 23 of the city of Kalinin [now Tver', its original name] sent an album to Aleksandr Pavlovich. It was inscribed as follows: "Our 'Ina Konstantinova' squad studying, working, and resting." A letter was included with the album as follows: "Dear Aleksandr Pavlovich! Please accept our modest gift. Leafing through the album, you will see how we live and study. Our squad was named after your daughter Ina. We shall do our utmost to behave in a manner befitting recipients of this honour."

There are many such letters. You read them as a most remarkable historical record. And once again you become convinced: heroes don't die. Not only because they are remembered forever, but because they actually live through us: through our deeds, our behaviour, and our thoughts. Ina found immortality through the lives of thousands of people.[3]

V.I. Gorbach, a former partisan, writes:

"The period which I spent with Aleksandr Pavlovich [Ina's father] and Ina was both the most difficult one and most rewarding for me, in terms of the wonderful memories. The difficult fighting conditions behind enemy lines drew us very close to one another. I very much respected and liked Aleksandr Pavlovich and considered myself a true friend of Ina. They took the place of my family, from whom I had no news of any kind for two years. I was proud of them both. Everyone liked and respected them, not only for their bravery, but also because of their marvellous spiritual qualities.

"Aleksandr Pavlovich had always served as a mentor and an example to me; and Ina was a friend with whom I could calmly go on any mission, even a most dangerous one, and with whom I could share my innermost thoughts and dreams. With Ina you could have the best heart-to-heart talk. With her, I could laugh, dream, and discuss all kinds of topics, as I couldn't do with anyone else.

"You just couldn't help but marvel at Ina's bravery at times. On some occasions...I privately admitted to myself that I wouldn't have been able to take some of the risks she took. Indeed, I was not the only one; everyone among our scouts felt the same. To run away from German captivity twice and courageously continue reconnoitring, without losing her nerve; this was genuine heroism."

Vadim Nikonenok joined Ina's detachment at fifteen. Ina, being older, exercised her right of "looking after him." The boy became as attached to Ina as if she were his own sister. He cried when he learned of her death. Here is his letter to Ina's parents:

"My dear Aleksandr Pavlovich and Vera Vasil'yevna:

"Your daughter Ina and I went out reconnoitring together. She used to come often to our village, even before I joined her detachment.

"When I joined the partisan detachment, Ina became a close friend to me. The first time I was sent reconnoitring, down the road between Kozukhi and Borki, where a movement of German troops had been detected, Ina took off her Nagant revolver, along with her Sam Browne belt, and handed them to me saying:

"'Vadik[4], you are walking on a military road. Take them; they might come handy.'

"When I returned, I gave the weapon back to her, thanking her. Then, two days later, I obtained a captured German rifle.

"After that I always went scouting with Ina. Usually, on the way she mentioned her family: mother, father, and younger sister Rena. She often talked about the future happy life she anticipated for herself. She was so eager to continue her education! In the detachment everyone liked and respected her very much....

"Ina was a remarkable comrade-in-arms. In combat she always pulled her own weight, shared hardships with men equally, and was always ready to help those who were weaker than herself and protect them from danger.

"She was strong-spirited, undaunted, and nothing stopped her, neither summer rain, nor winter snow, storm, and frost. When she saw how the Nazis were beating and killing our people, jabbing children with bayonets, and destroying property, she swore to avenge all this, even at the cost of her life. She kept her oath till the end, like a true Komsomol.

Vadim Nikonenok."

NOTES

1. A junior branch of the Komsomol (Young Communist League) for children aged ten to fourteen.
2. It is unlikely that such rituals continue in contemporary Russia.
3. Ina Konstantinova has likely been forgotten.
4. Diminutive of "Vadim."

Fig. 11. Masha Poryvayeva

PART II

MASHA'S BIRCH-TREES

N.V. Masolov[1]

By the Campfire

It was an early fall. On one occasion, after an unsuccessful hunt, I was spending the night on the shore of Yasskiy Lake. The weather was poor. The surface of the lake was wrinkled, and the splashing of the waves reminded me of the murmur of the sea. It was already close to midnight when I heard footsteps in the wind-fallen wood. An old man with a simple fishing-tackle on his back came up to the campfire.

"Doggone, I fell into a bog," the stranger said, instead of greeting me. He looked around and added softly: "I was looking for my boat. I noticed the campfire, so I came to dry myself beside it."

The old man, whose name turned out to be Ivan Yerofeyevich, said this in a friendly and appealing, deep voice. I invited him to while away the night beside the fire. A purple cloud moved in our direction from beyond the lake. The old man, ignoring the approaching storm, proceeded to hang out his wet clothing on wooden pegs. I couldn't resist asking him whether he was not afraid to face a storm in the woods.

"What is there to be afraid of? Everything here is familiar to us, my son. These are our native parts. Both the woods and the mountain will hide you in case of need."

"The mountain, too?"

"Yes, even the mountain," replied the old man. "During the troubled times, when the Nazis trampled our land, I once happened to go beyond Dedovichi: the devils sent me there with a wagon train. There is a mountain in that area, called Sudoma. I was told that sometimes the accursed enemy pinned partisans to its steep slopes; the wounded and exhausted partisans had nowhere else to go. It seemed they were doomed, but this was not meant to happen! During the night a noisy wind would blow up, like today, lightning would flash, and the mountain would open up. A punitive detachment would start out in the morning to finish off the partisans, but by that time they would disappear without a trace. Sudoma would have sheltered them."

As he was relating this, Ivan Yerofeyevich became completely transformed; he looked much younger than his seventy-five years. Sparks flashed in his faded eyes from time to time, resembling June bugs in woods at night.

We sat in silence for a few minutes, listening to the noise of the forest. "It's moaning like the Krasnoye birch-trees," the old man broke the silence.

"Tell me, about them, Ivan Yerofeyevich."

"These birch-trees were washed with a young girl's blood, my son. It happened almost twenty years ago. The Nazis went on a rampage in our area in 1942. They spared neither young nor old. The people became melancholy. Just then this very girl appeared in our Pustoshka woods. Her name was Zoya. The peasant women were saying that she was beautiful and had big eyes that were as crystal clear as the springs shooting up at the source of Velikaya River. She was supposedly sent from Moscow.

"She went from village to village and told the people about the fighting at the front, and she noted everything about the Nazi troops advancing toward Leningrad. She was followed by her detachment; it consisted partly of Red Army men and partly of partisans. And the boys and girls were all very young and reckless. The Germans called the detachment 'Red Airborne Assault Force.' Oh, how they feared it, especially the doggoned Nazi lackeys, the village elders and all kinds of policemen. And our people took heart; they began breathing easier. So then, the German chief, Kreser from Opochka, ordered that Zoya be captured. She probably wouldn't have been caught but for the intervention of a traitor who collaborated with the Nazis....

"In the early morning, she was led through Krasnoye, her hands tied behind her back, smiling at the sun and the people. And beside the Krasnoye birch-trees which grow by the lake on a slope, she shook her shoulders, threw off her fetters, grabbed an officer's submachine gun, and shot the monster. But the brave bird was not allowed to fly away; the enemy wounded her.

"The thrice-accursed, vile creatures tortured her in Opochka for a long time. They kept asking her all about her comrades and Moscow. But she stayed silent or sang a song. And then Kreser killed the girl, and threw her body into a God-forsaken swamp.

"Since that time, peasant women consider our Krasnoye birches a kind of Zoya's grave. Believe it or not, my son, but the birch-trees are moaning in bad weather. The women keep saying then: 'Zoya is summoning her friends to her grave'!"

Tired out by his tale, Ivan Yerofeyevich silently fingered his fishing tackle beside the dying campfire. I quietly got up from the pile of pine branches on which I was sitting, and went to the lake, to a spot from which the Velikaya ran out. Many years ago, Zoya the scout crossed the river in this area and walked toward Krasnoye.

Beyond the lake, with the first rays of yet invisible sun, the sky was turning pink. It was then that I decided to follow in the tracks of this young girl who had become a legend, in order to find her former comrades-in-arms and her loved ones, and to bring them all to the cherished birch-trees.

Zoya's True Identity

The answers which I received to my initial queries were not encouraging. The archivists whom I approached either could not tell me whether the story was true or asked for additional information. I persisted; finally, I was rewarded by a gleam of hope: in one of the documents of the Kalinin Party Archives, a similar occurrence to that of Zoya's capture, during a raid by the 2nd Kalinin Partisan Brigade, was recorded; yet the girl's name was not Zoya but Mariya [diminutive, Masha] and she supposedly killed a Nazi officer during her interrogation at a field gendarmerie.

I knew that the partisans were led on this raid, from the banks of the Volga to those of the Velikaya, by three brave and courageous men. The commander of the Brigade, Senior Lieutenant Arbuzov, was killed in an engagement during the raid; and its commissar Lekomtsev disappeared without a trace in 1944, after he transferred to the regular army.

The only survivor was the third man, Petr Ryndin, former commander of one of the Brigade's detachments [who replaced Arbuzov]. An address of his parents, dating to the early months of the war, was preserved in the Archives.

After a few more queries I received a letter from a certain official named Rebenko, Secretary of the Party Bureau of Temizhbekskiy Mill No. 15. He informed me as follows: "Mariya Kuz'minichna Ryndina (with a married surname Sergeyeva), who works at our mill, told me that her grandfather had lived in their village at the beginning of the war. Both his sons fought with the partisans: Kuz'ma (Mariya's father) was killed, but Petr is alive and lives in Vinnitsa Region."

In the course of my investigation I went though old newspapers and examined the published memoirs of partisans who had fought behind enemy lines, in the rear of enemy troops besieging Leningrad. I was sure I had come across the name Arbuzov in one of these sources. I was right; on re-reading the diary of partisan Ina Konstantinova, I found references there to Arbuzov. In a letter to her younger sister[2], Ina had written: "Renochek, I've something to ask of you: please find, among my letters, the one in which I wrote down the address of Zoya Poryvayeva. And keep it. Zoya was one of my best friends in the Brigade. What a remarkable girl! And she died a hero's death.... I am taking this very hard, Renochek. I intend to avenge them, motivated as I am by a terrible hatred!"

I was excited when I was entering an apartment in an old building in Moscow, the address of which I obtained from Konstantinova's letter.

"Did you say the name of the girl was Zoya Poryvayeva? Perhaps you mean Masha Poryvayeva? She did live here before the war. Her parents are dead, but her sister and brother, Mikhail Grigor'yevich, are alive. The brother works at an accordion factory in Moscow."

I had the urge to cover the woman with kisses for saying all this to me. My intuition prompted me to assume that Zoya's real name was Masha. But something troubled me: Konstantinova's letter mentioned Zoya Vasil'yevna Poryvayeva, whereas the Archives referred to Mariya Grigor'yevna Poryvayeva.

And then Poryvayeva's brother gave me her photograph. I examined the snapshot; so this was the legendary Masha. I sent it to Petr Vasil'yevich Ryndin, now a retired lieutenant-colonel, and his wife, Nina Ivanovna. (The latter had been a Komsomol regional committee instructor in organizing underground cells on Nazi-occupied Soviet territory.) In about a week, the photograph came back from Vinnitsa; the Ryndins wrote to me: "Yes, this is our Zoya!"

So the young girl who had become a legend was indeed named Masha. One of two daughters of a furnace man, Grigoriy Il'ich Poryvayev, she lived on Domnikovka Street in Moscow with her family and was a student at School No. 274 of the capital.

Since her early childhood, Masha dreamed about flying. She could sit for hours beside a window, her face supported on her little fists, looking at the rapidly moving clouds. Her girlfriend Vera would come up to her, hug her, and ask: "You want to fly away, Mashen'ka?" And Masha would blush and whisper to her: "The birds are so lucky; I envy them their wings."

Vera Il'inichna Vostrikova (Masha's girlfriend) recalled: "Mashen'ka was popular with her classmates; it was impossible not to like her; she was so kind and sympathetic. Yet the girls considered her a bit odd. During our elementary school years, we carried dolls in our school bags along with our exercise books. Masha, however, was interested solely in paper kites. Once she released a kite through a window and got so carried away in playing with it that she almost fell out. I barely managed to grab her legs. Also, she was friendly with the boys. When they started a fight, she would ran up to them. She would separate the antagonists and without saying a word would just stand there and smile. And the boys obeyed her. When we were older, we often went to a park, where everyone stood close to the platform on which couples were dancing, but Masha spent literally hours beside a parachute training jump tower, watching parachutists jump."

Masha was about thirteen when she went to a military recruitment office and blurted out: "I want to train as a pilot!" The recruitment officer, while escorting her to the door, said to her kindly: "You are a little too young to apply. Wait a bit."

Several years later, in the summer of 1940, on a sunny morning, a glider soared from an airfield outside Moscow. It was controlled by 18-year-old Masha Poryvayeva, glider pilot 1st Class.

In that same year, in No. 10 issue of *Smena* [Relief] magazine, appeared two snapshots with captions: "Marusya Poryvayeva preparing for a flight and being tasked by her instructor Rudakova" and "After circling once, Marusya Poryvayeva is making a landing approach." Beside the photographs, the magazine included a short article written by the enthusiastic glider pilot herself. Here is an excerpt from this article: "Below, under the wings of the glider, Moscow River is sparkling. Wide boulevards, straight as arrows, run in various directions. Here is the Theatre of the Red Army looking like a huge snow-white star. And here are green clumps of trees. How beautiful is Moscow [from the air]! You hate to tear yourself away from it."[3]

Soldier and Partisan

A slender young girl, wearing a Red Army field service cap and a close fitting field shirt, made one more effort, a jump across the ditch, and once again she heard the nasty bullet whistle over her head. Now she was safe! She ran into a field of rye; then she stopped for an instance and fell into the thick rye as if cut down by a submachine-gun burst.

Her pursuers gave up the chase. A short, stocky German in an officer's uniform swore malevolently, a grimace on his plain, pimpled face. Then, without taking aim, he fired his parabellum gun in the direction of the field and, looking around apprehensively, walked rapidly toward his vehicle parked beside the highroad. The soldier who accompanied him opened the car door obsequiously.

It was drizzling. The rain fell monotonously in tiny drops, as if put through a fine sieve. The unreaped rye bent sadly to the ground, as if complaining about the farmers who had forgotten to cut it down with their sharp sickles.

Ignoring the rain, Masha (for she was the young woman who had just escaped an almost certain death) lay motionless on the crushed stems for a long time. Her uniform was soaked through; she had a burning sensation in her chest; and her lips were dry.

For almost a week, after her volunteer [?] regiment formed in Moscow was decimated, Masha made her way back to Moscow along the Old Smolensk Road. She was accompanied by Mikhail, an 18-year-old youth, shy, red-cheeked, the down on his upper lip looking ridiculous, and an older man named Petr Vasil'yevich, who was over forty. A former seaman of the Baltic Fleet, he was broad-shouldered and stooping. Wounded in the left shoulder during his unit's final battle, he walked with considerable difficulty.

They made their way at night. In daytime, they hid in copses and abandoned houses. That morning they stopped in a semi-demolished shed near the highroad. Worn out by hunger and exhaustion, Masha and Petr Vasil'yevich immediately fell asleep. Mikhail, who was keeping watch, soon fell asleep too. The seaman, a light sleeper, was the first to hear foreign speech by the shed's door: "Get up! *Schnell! Schnell!*"

The Germans entered the shed accidentally, in search of boards to free their vehicle, which was stuck in the mud.

Urged by the Germans, the three Soviet soldiers pulled out the Oppel. The officer grinned: "Your Moscow is *kaput!* Today I'll reach Moscow, and enjoy its girls and vodka. And as for you, you ought to be grateful; say 'thank you'!"

Almost simultaneously, he fired twice at Petr Vasil'yevich and then took aim at Poryvayeva. "Run, Masha!" screamed Mikhail, covering her with his body. The officer, scared by the youth's sudden jump, withdrew to one side, and this saved the girl.

Masha was prone, pressing herself to the ground. Images from recent past flashed trough her mind. A small room on Domnikovka; in one corner, partitioned off by a blanket, she was doing her homework, while a cousin kept mumbling: "Masha, eh, Mash, tell me more about Chkalov!"[4]

Then she was running through a field toward her glider. She took off, the blue sky was all around her, and Moscow under the wings. It seemed to her that this had happened so long ago! .

She was awakened by a loud noise; tanks rolled along the highroad. The tanks interrupted her daydreaming. The present seemed terrible and gloomy; and she dreaded the possibility that Moscow had surrendered. The chill forced her to act. Afflicted by a strange, persistent trembling, she began to crawl. Then she got up beside a clump of bushes and subsequently plodded along in the direction opposite to the highroad. She decided to go south; possibly she might break through to Khar'kov, where her older sister Valentina lived.

For two days Masha wandered, by-passing all the settlements on her way. She was feverish from lying on dump ground, and her legs were swollen. Very hungry, on the third day she managed to enter a big house on the outskirts of one village, and asked for some bread. But the master of the house showed her the door. This upset her so much she almost burst out crying. Then she started walking along the street leading to the village school.

The stone building seemed huge in the twilight; the cavities of the broken windows made her fearful. Something was suspended from a horizontal bar on the playground. Masha approached it and jumped back. A body of a woman was swinging from a rope.

"Our teacher!" Masha turned around and saw a little girl with a turned up nose. "I followed you. Grandfather Nikanor ordered me to do it. As soon as it gets dark, go to the house in an orchard!" She pointed toward the river and disappeared just as suddenly as she had appeared to Masha.

Later on Masha found it difficult to recall how she reached the little house in an orchard. She told everything feverishly to Nikanor Ivanovich, an old beekeeper with a kind, pitted face, while drinking a glass of scalding tea with honey. And she cried from joy when she learned that the Nazi officer had lied when he boasted that Moscow had been taken.

Masha rested for two days and two nights at the old beekeeper's house. The old man gave her a lot of good advice, while she warmed herself by his stove, the fall wind moaning in the chimney. He suggested that she stay with his sister in an adjacent village. But Masha made a firm decision to break through to Moscow. Nikanor Ivanovich provided her with a passport with a German seal, issued to a peasant woman Agrafena Sharoyko (the name of his late relative), who had lived in the town of Serpukhov and had allegedly been incarcerated by the Soviets and freed by the Germans.

Already the golden leaves were falling, whirling in the wind; a silvery hoarfrost covered the fields in the morning. But Masha kept walking, swimming across rivers, and crossing treacherous marshes. Hungry, she hid in dense hazelnut bushes for days at a time. The document, obtained by Nikanor Ivanovich, rescued her on several occasions.

Once she was detected by an enemy patrol. The soldiers, accompanied by dogs, pursued her to a village near the front, where she was taken prisoner. The enemy troops were rounding up Soviet women, to select those suitable for brothels. In a former club, the women were subjected to a humiliating inspection. When Masha's turn came, a Russian doctor looked her over and said to a middle-aged German captain: "Too thin; nothing but skin and bones." Masha was assigned the task of spying for the police on the women. She pretended she was willing to do this and became upset when one of the Soviet women called her a "traitor."

However, Masha's career as a police informer was to end almost immediately. Unexpectedly, Red Army units broke through to the village two days later. Meanwhile, a colonel had arrived from the HQ of a German division and ordered the local German commandant to build defensive works immediately, using 200 Russians. Taking advantage of the ensuing confusion, Masha climbed into one of the trucks which had arrived to transport the Russians. They hauled stones to the highway, where earth-and-timber emplacements were being built, until dark. For some reason the trucks failed to come back in the evening. That night, Masha, among others, managed to run away.

When emaciated, her face wind-burnt, she finally rejoined her family in Moscow, her mother and brother at first didn't recognize her, she was so mature and stern-looking. Clearly, in a short time she lived through and learned as much as others might live and learn over a period of many years.

Her rest at home was brief. She was anxious to square her account with the enemy and to repay him for the demolished towns and villages she had seen while wandering through the occupied territory, for the brutal murder of Misha and Petr Vasil'yevich, and for the teacher swinging from a horizontal bar at the playground. So Masha volunteered for work behind enemy lines, and was trained as a partisan scout and an operative.

In the spring of 1942, when the streams began to gurgle beside the roads, Poryvayeva, under the code name Zoya, was sent to a very important area, the so-called "railway triangle," formed by the stations at Nevel',

Novosokol'niki, and Velikiye Luki. She was to cross the front lines eight times, wandering near enemy airfields dressed as a beggar woman or travelling, disguised as a rich peasant woman on her way to a dressmaker, to several towns in which enemy garrisons were located.

The reconnaissance carried out by Masha Poryvayeva jointly with her fellow female scout Dusya Tsvetova provided the Brigade commander Arbuzov and the pertinent army command echelon with a great deal of interesting and valuable data. The girls were both bold and careful. On one occasion they tested their disguise on the sentry guarding the Brigade's HQ. This took place just before their departure for the town of Nevel' with a carefully fabricated story. They assumed the identity of refugee women whose German passports were issued at Vitebsk, and the partisan sentry failed to recognize them and refused to let them pass.

Once, near Nevel', Masha appropriated a map case, belonging to an amorous German staff officer, which contained operational documents of a Nazi tank division. This caused a great deal of rejoicing in Petr Ryndin's "For Our Native Land" partisan detachment, then based in the small village of Kupuy. Masha had scored this success on the second day of her mission, after obtaining a great deal of intelligence at the station at Opukhliki. She learned that a battalion of armoured trains was indeed based there; the platforms with guns had stood on a branch line, camouflaged with special nets. A week earlier, the battalion in question had unexpectedly departed for Polotsk. Masha proved unable to determine the reason for this transfer. However, she overheard that the battalion was expected to return shortly. Consequently, she decided to come back to the station; here she made a mistake which resulted in a brilliant finale.

Masha noticed several women reading the text of a piece of paper attached to a fence. When she came closer, she discovered it was a Soviet leaflet, secured to the boards with thumbtacks. She began to read it, but suddenly realized she was all alone; the women had disappeared. Sensing that someone was approaching, Masha nevertheless didn't look behind her. For a few seconds she stared at the leaflet; she then ripped it off in a temper, sharply turned around, and said: "What an outrage!"

A German *Oberleutnant*, accompanied by an intoxicated policeman, stood two paces away from her. She noticed that the officer was showing the effects of the consumed alcohol even more than the policeman did. The German, suitably impressed by her behaviour and shapely figure, offered to take her to Nevel' in a handcar. On the way, the officer felt ill, and ordered the handcar stopped. Then Masha helpfully suggested that they take a rest and picnic in a nearby grove. Here she put him to sleep with a glass of home-brew. She then stole his map case and ran away.

Tat'yana Prokhorova, a former scout now residing in Pushkinskiye Gory, recalls: "In the morning of... [28 July], Masha and I went to the Lovat' to rinse out our laundry. Zoya walked beside me, shining with joy, and told me mischievously: 'You know, Tanyukha, I've become very strong. And do you know why? I learned how to hide my feelings during my encounters with the enemy. The day before yesterday, a Nazi Oberleutnant and a drunk policeman approached me. The latter had bloodshot eyes and gave me a poke in the ribs with his submachine gun; he accused me of being a partisan. And I, without looking at him, turned to the officer, called him "captain," and asked him to check my documents, insisting that I had to join my aunt in Nevel'. I was smiling as I was talking. The officer brightened up, called me *Fraulein*, and offered to take me to Nevel' in a handcar and treat me to a meal in a restaurant. On the way, I managed to get hold of his map case'."

[Masha continued]: "When I was in training, the instructor, a captain, kept saying: 'An agent's task is not easy. You have to know a great deal and master many skills, but the ability to hide your feelings from the enemy is paramount. If necessary, you play at give-away with him: you smile and you flirt with him.' I listened and I thought: Not on your life! I won't do it; it is enough that in 1941 I was once called a 'traitor' by a compatriot. But I did follow the captain's instructions out of a sense of duty. All the same" — and, according to Prokhorova, Masha smiled crookedly: "you've no idea how I hate to be taken for a Nazi's girlfriend. But I really enjoyed myself when I saw how the vile policeman grovelled at my feet."

In July 1942 the Brigade had set off for the Pustoshka, Kudever, and Idritsa Districts, in order to "ignite the flame of partisan warfare." This raid was so daring that the Nazis mistook the partisans for an airborne assault force. In carrying out his mission, Arbuzov was assisted by a number of female scouts. Among them was Masha Poryvayeva.

On her final mission, Masha's destination was the large village of Shchukino. The boundary of Kudever District, as well as the road leading to the important town of Opochka, ran beside it. The interested Soviet army command echelon suspected that a large garrison of German security troops was stationed at the strategically located Shchukino. Masha's task was to investigate the situation in the village.

For a time, the Germans left the Brigade in peace. On 6 August, the detachments named "For Our Native Land" and "People's Avenger" entered the forest to the north-west of Shchukino. Here, near a beautiful small lake, they made a camp. A vague, barely perceptible uneasiness took hold of Arbuzov, when his chief of staff Petr Kotlyarov reported that neither Poryvayeva nor Konstantinova were waiting at the appointed place, even though the Brigade was one day late in arriving in the area. What prevented Masha, always so punctual, from returning on time?

Masha had a great deal of luck at the beginning; she reached the vicinity of Shchukino relatively quickly and without encountering any obstacles. Her initial careful inquiries confirmed what Arbuzov had suspected all along; there was a large garrison in the village, which happened to be a base for several punitive detachments. In addition, Nazi administrative echelons were stationed nearby. Masha decided not to go to Shchukino immediately, but to approach it gradually, by-passing the villages in its vicinity. The last such village on her itinerary was Krasnoye.

It was beginning to get dark when, on her way to Krasnoye, she came to a village called Ivakhnevo, where a friendly peasant woman offered to put her up for the night, without asking any questions. Masha inquired: "May I sleep in the shed on top of the hay?"

"Why not? Go ahead, if you are not afraid to sleep there by yourself. Have some milk before going to bed."

It was quiet on the village street, so Masha couldn't resist the urge to stand outside for a while before going to bed, to enjoy the night and to mentally visit her home on her dear Domnikovka Street. Lost in reverie, the girl barely noticed a cyclist going by and casting an unfriendly glance at her. Thus, this man, who worked for the army of occupation as a clerk and interpreter, accidentally learned where she was spending the night.

Masha got up at dawn, while a thick mist was still rising from the ground, thanked the landlady for her hospitality, and slowly walked toward Krasnoye. Its two-storey school building loomed ahead. Masha came out onto the road leading to the school. Suddenly, while she was passing an old smithy, a menacing "Halt!" rang out.

Three men ran out from behind a corner: a private, an officer, and a red-haired civilian. Masha noticed that the officer was an SS-man. Handing her passport to the officer, she said: "I am a poor *Fraulein*, who had come from far away, and suddenly — such a reception!"

"Some *Fraulein*," teased her the civilian (it was the cyclist who had seen her the night before). "We know who you are."

"Hold your tongue; I am talking to an officer," retorted Masha angrily. "And do translate everything; I know some German."

The SS-man liked the way the stranger cut the interpreter Pavel [Paul] off. (Paul happened to be a Russified German.) Masha's passport seemed in order. The officer returned it to her, joking coarsely, and she pretended to enjoy his company. Walking together, they reached a group of large birch-trees with branches overhanging the cart-road. It was from here that the SS-man sent his two companions away. Masha understood that the interpreter was to get milk and the soldier was ordered to fetch a horse. She grew alarmed. Were they planning to take her to Shchukino? The officer sat down on a mound, opposite the birch-trees, and placed his submachine gun between his legs. He offered her a cigarette. She refused, racking her brain as to what she should do.

An opportunity to act presented itself to her suddenly, as the officer brought both his hands to his face while lighting his cigarette. So she dashed toward him, bent over, and grabbed his weapon. Then she jumped back a few paces and fired a long burst at the SS-man, who by this time had managed to get up. As she was starting to run two rifle shots rang out behind her, fired by the returning interpreter.

Ahead of her, beyond a small field covered with camomile, was a forest. If only she could reach it! But a German road patrol consisting of three soldiers suddenly appeared on the scene. Poryvayeva stopped, raised the gun, and pulled the trigger. She expected to fire a burst; instead a single shot rang out. Apparently the officer forgot to replace the magazine.

This turned out to be the brave girl's undoing. An enemy bullet pierced her hand, and her pursuers caught up with her. Swearing, they dragged her toward the birch-trees, where the officer lay in a cart, mortally wounded by eight bullets. Subsequently she was beaten with rifle butts, kicked with army boots, bound with reins, and then led to Shchukino behind the cart.

The Interrogation

The HQ of the German garrison at Shchukino was located on the premises of the village's hospital. After the punitive expedition arrived in the village in the fall of 1941 terrible things had been happening in the building with an iron roof, and decent people avoided it. Only a few renegades, including the clerk who betrayed Masha, and two criminals whose surnames were unknown, Vit'ka and Yurka, visited the HQ of the occupying force.

Here the "chief" (the punitive force referred thus to their commander) interrogated captured Red Army servicemen as well as partisans and other members of the Resistance. Those who were arrested were sent to the town of Opochka, where their cases became of interest to the Gestapo and the SS security service, or to the "hole," i.e. a big ditch in the park. In the first instance, the victim went to the gallows, and in the second, the prisoner received a bullet in the back of his or her head.

The "chief" had a great many lives on his conscience. None of the local inhabitants knew the surname of the tow-haired 40-year-old German with a high peaked cap, always pulled over his forehead, and an iron cross on his shabby uniform. However, his evil reputation spread far beyond the local villages.

It was this officer who brought to Shchukino about forty elderly scientists, engineers, and teachers, captured in a sanatorium near Leningrad in the fall of the first year of the war. The details of the savage treatment they were subjected to became known only recently. Emaciated and sick, they were locked up in a building ironically referred to as the "nursing home." Local citizens were forbidden, under pain of death, to approach the dungeon, from which terrible moans issued at night. The wretches were left there to rot....

In the morning, around the time Masha appeared in Krasnoye, the "chief" sent an additional patrol toward the road. Then he called up Lieutenant Haase, the commander of the logistical unit located in the vicinity of Krasnoye, and sounded an alarm. The day before, in the evening, Captain Kreser, SS section chief, had rung up from Opochka, warning that a "Red Airborne Assault Force" had landed in the vicinity of Pustoshka.

On the way to Shchukino Masha lost a great deal of blood. When finally her hands were untied and her wound was dressed, she almost blacked out. The "chief" noticed this, and began to interrogate her immediately. Paul, the red-haired civilian, acted as an interpreter. As soon as he saw how furious the "chief" was, Paul, shaking with fear at the thought that Kreser might find out about his absence as the girl fired at the officer, stopped acting offhand. To the intimidating questions posed by the "chief," he added his own solemn pledges to spare her life should she reveal the whereabouts of the "Red Airborne Assault Force."

Masha kept silent, and only when the "chief" threatened to burn down Krasnoye, unless she named her relatives in the village, stated firmly: "No one knows me here. I am from Moscow."[5]

"*Donner veter...Moskau!*" yelled the "chief," kicking Masha in the stomach. The girl gasped, and as she was falling chest forward onto his desk, noticed a handy bronze paperweight; she picked it up, raised herself, and threw it at her tormentor. The blow caught him just above his left eye. The "chief" cried out in agony.

In the late afternoon Masha regained consciousness in a wooden shed, where she had been locked up after a brutal beating had been administered to her. Suddenly something fell to the floor. It was a sickle with a rolled up cover of an exercise book attached to the handle. Masha crawled toward the sickle, picked it up, and unrolled the piece of paper. On it a five-pointed star was drawn in a child's hand; the message read: "Run to the forest tonight." It was signed simply: "A Young Pioneer."

Alas, she couldn't avail herself of the tiny patriot's assistance! After her evening interrogation, she was kept at the HQ overnight. But his selfless act was not in vain, for Masha took heart and went to face her tormentors with a proudly uplifted head.

And the torments she had to endure were most brutal and cruel. When the twilight descended onto the village, Masha was transferred to the operating room. Rolling up his sleeves in a businesslike fashion and grinning repulsively, the "chief" tore the clothing off the girl, and with the aid of the interpreter tied her to the operating table. Employing surgical instruments from a handy cabinet, he now plunged a scalpel and now a syringe into her back, asking repeatedly: "Where are your comrades? Who is in command of the detachment? Are you going to tell me, or not?"

All she had to do was to say one word, and he would stop torturing her. Yet to start talking was tantamount to betraying her comrades-in-arms who believed in her, and would have shared their last piece of bread with her. Half-conscious from pain, in her mind's eye she probably saw, one after another, the faces of her brave girlfriends — Ina Konstantinova, Tanya Prokhorova, Nina Salazko, and Vera Bocharova, among others.... Sometimes, it seemed to her that they were near, looking at her, and that tears ran down the cheeks of Yulya Novoselova, the stern partisan doctor. Masha kept peering into space, but all she saw was a medicine cabinet, and the letters on the cabinet reading "Medications" now came near and now floated away.

When her back was transformed into a single wound, she whispered: "I'll tell...." Her tormentors were pleased; they untied her and gave her a glass of cold water to drink. In one gulp, she emptied it. Then she screamed to the top of her voice, so that the women who were cleaning the adjoining rooms could hear her: "Good-bye, comrades! Death to German invaders!"

The Unfinished Song

After waiting in vain for Poryvayeva and Konstantinova, Arbuzov decided to cross the railway track and to advance along the assigned route. The detachment marched all night. At dawn, they stopped and encamped for the day. To the left of the partisan bivouac flashed a small lake; a path, overgrown with ferns, ran about 100 metres from the shore. About noon, a peasant woman carrying a purse appeared on the road, and the sentries stopped her. The woman told the partisans what had happened to Masha.

"The Germans have gone mad," said the woman. "My sister told me that yesterday they caught a young woman, supposedly called Zoya, in the vicinity of the village of Shchukino. They administered a terrible beating to the poor thing. Apparently, she will be driven to Opochka tomorrow." When they heard this, the partisans begged Arbuzov to give them an order to attack Shchukino.

But the Senior Lieutenant couldn't issue such an order; the detachment was too weak to raid Shchukino. Also, the numerical strength of the Shchukino enemy garrison was not known. In addition, the enemy had increased his vigilance. This was confirmed by scouts Tanya Prokhorova and Varya Kaftyreva, on returning from their reconnoitring. The girls were assigned a mission to make contacts in the village of Maksimtsevo, but had been ambushed and Prokhorova was wounded. "There is an ambush set up on every road," they reported.

After consulting with his detachment commanders, Ryndin and Lesnikov, Arbuzov issued an order to advance. He sent an assault group ahead, to set up an ambush beside the road connecting Shchukino and Glubokoye, along which Masha would be driven to Opochka.

However, the attempt to rescue her failed, for the following reason. A wagon train left Shchukino in the late afternoon, escorted by trucks filled with German soldiers. Masha, her arms and legs tied, lay in the body of one of the trucks. The column was already under way when Kreser rang up the "chief" and ordered him to deliver Masha personally. The commander of the punitive force jumped into his car, caught up with the column, and grabbed Poryvayeva. The partisans, assuming that Poryvayeva was being driven in a truck, let the car go by, so as not to unmask the ambush. They smashed the column, but Masha fell into Kreser's clutches.

The Captain didn't like witnesses during his interrogations, with the exception of the interpreter. He was fond of comfortable furniture and usually conducted his interrogations reclining on a couch. He would get up only to deliver a blow. During the interrogation of Poryvayeva, this routine was going to be upset, for she was to be examined first by the counter-intelligence agent Gorbunov. Kreser couldn't stand this Russian, but was afraid of him. The son of a former Pskov landlord who had been a Tsarist military attaché, Gorbunov had served as an officer under Yudenich during the Civil War [1918-1921] and was highly thought of at the HQ of Army Group "North."

When Masha, half-dead, was escorted into the office of the investigator, Kreser was furious. He had just been informed that the officer at whom Masha had fired had died of his wounds. On the other hand, Gorbunov couldn't care less about this. The "Red Airborne Assault Force" was virtually of no interest to him. He was anxious to learn, from the arrested woman, something about the secret service operating in the rear area of the Nazi troops in the vicinity of Leningrad!

"Well, young lady, you and I don't need an interpreter," began Gorbunov. "We are compatriots and colleagues. I believe your name is Zoya. As you know, Zoya, when a spy gets caught he or she is invariably presented with a choice: to die or to exchange an employer. I am prepared to give you a guarantee that your life will be spared, provided you reply to my questions truthfully. You will then receive medical treatment and we shall work together...." Here Gorbunov hesitated and then concluded with enthusiasm: "For the benefit of Russia!"

Gorbunov saw tears in Masha's eyes and must have observed mentally: "She gave in so quickly." So, trying to be kind, he continued: "No need to cry. You are so young. Unfortunately, we have but one life. I don't wish to hurry you. You can tell me everything tomorrow."

"No need to wait till tomorrow," interjected Masha. "Let's settle the matter today. Do you think, Judas, that my tears indicate that I am sorry to have to die so young? No! I am crying because I am now incapable of killing you, you Nazi!"

When Kreser heard the word "Nazi" being uttered, he joined Gorbunov. "Enough of that Bolshevist nonsense, Mr. Gorbunov. She ought to be given a beating."

"I believe you're right, Captain," replied Gorbunov, throwing up his hands. "She refuses to talk."

It was now Kreser's turn to interrogate Masha. The sky slowly paled outside the window. In a few minutes, the crimson strip of dawn would be ushering a new day. Masha knew: this would be her last morning. In the common cell people were saying that Kreser ordered all executions to be scheduled in the morning. So they will execute her today. What day was it? 13 August? A year ago she left Moscow, her dear home town. Undoubtedly, Moscow streets were still blacked out. But a time will come when a multitude of lights will again adorn the city squares as well as the embankments of Moscow River, and again the Kremlin stars will shine in the sky.

Masha tried to move. An agonizing pain pierced her entire body. Her back felt as if on fire. Her wounded hand felt heavy as if made of lead. Heavy strides were heard above the cellar which served as the jail cell, and the door opened with an unpleasant squeak. With a stream of fresh air came the order: "Come out!"

Thirty paces from the building, by the wall of a shed, two human bodies were swinging from the gallows. Beside them hung a piece of rope.

Well-groomed, clean-shaven, his hair flattened and combed back, Kreser advanced toward her. He looked as if he was going to a parade. "The High Command decided to hang you, wench. You are not a soldier, but a bandit," barked Kreser.

Suddenly, Masha took a step toward Kreser and started singing:

> To thunder of a cannonade,
> We marched, looking death in the eye....

(While singing, Masha probably recalled how she had bitterly cried over the fate of the young drummer boy, the hero of the song, when she had heard it for the first time beside a Young Pioneer campfire.) Her gaze directed forward, her eyes aglow, she became truly beautiful in her final outburst. Broken by torture, her hands tied with barbed wire, the young woman partisan nevertheless proved stronger than her foes. Startled, Kreser stepped back one pace. Then he lost control over himself, pulled out his Browning from its holster, and fired twice into Poryvayeva's chest.

Behind him, he heard Gorbunov's sarcastic remark:" You can't take it, Captain; your nerves are giving you trouble!"

Kreser turned around. "What an accursed country!" he flung at the Russian involuntarily. Then he noticed the approaching executioner, pointed at Poryvayeva's body, and screamed, half-losing his voice: "Hang her! Hang her!"

Twenty Years Later

In the fall of 1961, after learning the details of their co-worker's death, the employees of the Red Army Accordion Factory in Moscow, where Masha had worked before the war, sent a special delegation to Pustoshka, which included her brother Mikhail.

Among those who came was Yulya Novoselova, Masha's former comrade-in-arms, as well as Yakov Vasil'yevich Vasil'yev, former Secretary of the Pustoshka Underground Party District Committee; and from distant Vinnitsa Region came Petr Vasil'yevich Ryndin, who had replaced Arbuzov as commander of Masha's partisan brigade.

Fig. 11. From right to left: Ya. V. Vasil'yev, former Secretary of the Pustoshka Underground District Party Committee, and P.V. Ryndin, former commander of 2nd Kalinin Partisan Brigade, among Young Pioneers of Masha Poryvayeva School in Krasnoye.

And here we were at Krasnoye. Bugles of Young Pioneers summoned us; silence descended on Krasnoye School corridors; and Young Pioneers solemnly formed up in the auditorium and stood still.

The delegates from Moscow, Masha's former comrades-in-arms, teachers, and collective farm workers — all followed the streaming red banner with tear-filled eyes. Everybody was moved. Perhaps some recalled their troubled youth, their partisan campfires, and long-dead comrades whom they still mourned in their aching hearts.

The Young Pioneer Squad named after Masha Poryvayeva reported to Ye.P. Makeyenko, First Secretary of the Pustoshka District Party Committee. He was just as moved as the children and guests were. Then

Nina Fedorovna Nikitina, a collective farm worker, took the floor. "My dear children! I will never forget the morning when Masha, under the assumed name Zoya, went by your school. I was then a 13-years-old driving cows to pasture at dawn. Suddenly, I heard shots being fired...."

Lena Faynshtayn, Komsomol Secretary of the Accordion Factory, handed a large portrait of Masha to the Young Pioneers. "Thank you, young friends, on behalf of all of our Komsomol members, thank you for remembering our Masha," she said. And then, someone broke into a song. Everyone joined in the singing:

> Among us was a drummer boy,
> He led us in every attack....

We came out of the school. Near the oblong lake, the branches of the powerful birch-trees overhung the cart-road. At the foot of one of them was a post with a small, smooth board. The inscription on it read:

PARTISAN SCOUT MASHA PORYVAYEVA
WAS CAPTURED HERE BY GERMAN TROOPS
IN THE SUMMER OF 1942

Mikhail Grigor'yevich Poryvayev, his wife Vera Petrovna, and Yuliya Novoselova, who had given Masha a send-off before her fateful mission, bowed down toward the ground that had drunk the heroine's blood. For a long time we stood beside the memorial; then we went to the settlement of Shchukino.

The club of the collective farm was full of people. They came from far away, in order to pay homage to Masha, a young girl who had become a legend. Here both young and old listened attentively to Ryndin's story about the famous partisan raid. Then Yakov Vasil'yevich Vasil'yev talked about the exploits of some of the former Kalinin partisans: Podrezova, Novoselova, Kotlyarov, Maslenok, and Kozlov, among others.

Henrietta Bundzen, the daughter of a Leningrad area partisan, made the following pledge: "The days when this land was scorched by the flames of war recede farther and farther into the past. Yet, regardless of the number of years that might separate us from the bright V-Day, neither the distance nor the time can erase from people's memory the names of those who had sacrificed their lives — their most precious possession — at the Fatherland's altar. We will never forget Masha. She shall live in our labour and struggles, in our joys and sorrows, and in our memory and songs."

Nikolay Ivanovich Malyshev, Secretary of the Party Committee of the Accordion Factory, handed to Zakhar Pavlovich Shamanov, Chairman of the "Spring Sunbeam" Collective Farm, a gift from the Moscow delegation. "Masha Poryvayeva collected accordions and loved to sing. The workers asked me to give you an accordion made in our factory to remember her by."

It was late when we returned to Pustoshka. We felt both good and sad, as always happens during your encounters with the past, when such encounters are illuminated by a special spiritual light.... At the request of the Komsomol of the capital, Domnikovka was re-named Mariya Poryvayeva Street. Young Pioneer squads and detachments in Moscow, Leningrad, Velikiye Luki, Pskov, and Pustoshka have been named after her as well.

And then, a cherished dream of those who had formerly served under Arbuzov finally came true: to hold a reunion at Krasnoye, beside the birch-trees where Masha Poryvayeva's thorny path to immortality began. The unveiling of an obelisk to commemorate the feat of scout Masha Poryvayeva was attended by Ryndin, Fedyunina (neé Bakhenskaya), Dudushkin, Milyutina (née Bocharova), and Novikova (née Sharova); guests arrived from Moscow, Leningrad, Kalinin, and Pskov. Also came representatives of the state and collective farms in the District, as well as Young Pioneers from Pustoshka, Shchukino, Krasnoye, Alol', and Poddub'ye. About one thousand people gathered. Then followed the unveiling of the obelisk, followed by the salute. Suddenly, two voices — one male and one female — rang out in unison:

To thunder of a cannonade...

This was Sanya Aksenova, the leader of Pustoshka Komsomol, and Mikhail Alekseyevich Mikhanoshchenok, principal of Masha Poryvayeva School at Krasnoye, singing her favourite song. Young Pioneers, veterans, collective farm workers, participants of the "Red Airborne Assault Force" — all joined in. The voices grew stronger and more sonorous, resounding over the quiet village, the mirror-like surface of the lake, and the fertile fields:

The wartime years flashed by,
Ending the glorious campaign.
Perished our young drummer boy,
But the song about him lives on.

* * *

If you happen to be travelling in Pskov Region, reader, do visit Krasnoye, and come down to take a look at the birch-trees which are now called "Masha's little birches." When a blizzard is raging or a sudden gust of strong wind blows, the birch-trees bend, clinging to the very slope from which they had sprang, but they don't break. They defy both blizzard and wind, just like the brave partisan, who had stained the ground beneath them with her blood, had defied the cruel enemy many years ago.

NOTES

1.   Tayna Zoi Kruglovoy [The Secret of Zoya Kruglova]. Leningrad: Lenizdat, 1962, 72pp; and *Ballada o krasnom desante* [A Ballad about the Red Airborne Assault Force]. Moscow: Politizdat, 1967, 160pp. Nikolay Vissarionovich Masolov was born in 1915, in Pskov Region. He became a rural teacher in 1932, and between 1939 and 1960 served in the Baltic Fleet. His decorations for World War II service include the Orders of Patriotic War I and II Class, two Orders of the Red Banner, and several medals. War correspondent and author, N.V. Masolov graduated extramurally from the Pedagogical Institute in Smolensk and the Party School attached to its Central Committee. In addition to the above-mentioned books, he is the author of *Dnovskaya byl'* [The True Story of Dno]. Moscow: Politizdat, 1964, 87pp; *Neobychnyy reid* [Unusual Raid]. Moscow, Politizdat, 1972, 152pp; and *Za osobyye zaslugi* [For Rendering Special Services]. Moscow: Izdatel'stvo Politicheskoy Literatury, 1988, 94pp. As well, he edited and co-authored a number of other books about little known heroes of the Battle for Leningrad. See S.F. Vinogradova, etal., eds., *Leningradki. Vospominaniya, ocherki, dokumenty* [Women of Leningrad: Reminiscences, Sketches, and Documents] (Leningrad: Lenizdat, 1968), p. 408.

2.   Konstantinova's letter was dated 29 August 1942. See p. 57 of this book.

3.   Masolov, *Ballada*, p. 131.

4.   Famous pre-war pilot who died in 1938 while testing a fighter.

5.   Masolov, *Tayna*, p. 14. Vladimir Ivanovich Margo, a well-known partisan leader in the Leningrad area, maintained that it was essential for the partisans to have local population at their disposal. When the brigade commanded by Senior Lieutenant Georgiy Arbuzov raided Kudever, Pustoshka, and Idritsa Districts, there were no local inhabitants in its ranks, which was a serious handicap, that is, reconnaissance and new contacts took up too much of the Brigade's valuable time. See V.I. Margo, *Pylayushchiy les* [The Blazing Forest] (Leningrad: Lenizdat, 1970), p. 36, with Foreword by Marshal A.I. Yeremenko, former commander of the Kalinin Front (Army Group).

Fig. 12. Agent Zoya Baiger

PART III

THE SECRET OF ZOYA KRUGLOVA

N.V. Masolov[1]

The Inscription on Jail Wall

Named after an ancient fortress, Ostrov is an old Russian town, picturesquely sprawling on the banks of the Velikaya River. A southern outpost of Pskov Region, it has existed for over 500 years. During this period the town had withstood numerous raids and sieges, but the most severe trials befell it during the Nazi occupation.

On 4 July 1941 the enemy's dirty-green trucks and prime movers pulling artillery pieces entered Ostrov; the alien German language was henceforth spoken on its streets. For three long years, the Nazis did as they liked in this ancient Russian town, dealing brutally with its patriots. The Gestapo turned the Ostrov Jail into a terrible dungeon, where executioners in military uniforms starved and tortured prisoners. Those who spent their final hours in solitary confinement, awaiting execution, included partisans, members of urban Resistance, and former soldiers of the Leningrad Front (Army Group) who escaped from PoW camps. The messages inscribed by the prisoners on the walls of their cells are eloquent:

"Mila Filippova. Cell No. 24. I've been here since 23 August 1943. Today is 1 September 1943. The interrogations have ended. I was terribly beaten. I am all alone, awaiting my sentence. I believe I'll be shot, but nevertheless I want to live." ..."29 April. We dug another pit. Again we await execution.... Please give our warmest regards to our loved ones and the young people from the settlement of Vorontsovo. Farewell. Vera Andreyeva and Nyura Yermolayeva, girlfriends." Another inscription follows: "Nyura and Vera were shot on the 30th."

In Cell No. 23 an anonymous inscription reads: "A wounded partisan was kept here. Was shot. Died for his country." And beside it, there was another inscription: "I once so loved freedom, independence, open spaces, and therefore it is very difficult for me to get used to captivity. My name 'Zoya' means 'life' in Greek. Ah, how I want to live, live.... Zoya Baiger (Kruglova)."

"Ah, how I want to live...." So much human suffering is contained in these few words scratched on a stone wall! Who was this girl? Why did the

German jailers deprived her of freedom?

All kinds of things were being said about Zoya Baiger immediately after the war. It was alleged that she went out with German officers, and boldly danced at Nazi parties. Why then did the enemy imprison, torture, and execute Baiger? Why did the surname "Kruglova" appear in parentheses after "Baiger" on the stone wall? It was only thirteen years after the final shot was fired in Europe that Zoya's secret was revealed.

Zoya's Youth

Fedos'ya Kapitonovna Kruglova, Zoya's mother, took out a newspaper from a chest of drawers. "Here is a story about my children.... About Zoyen'ka when she was a Young Pioneer," she said quietly. The newspaper was more than 20-years-old and the paper had turned yellow. In a faded photograph, a girl with pigtails sat behind a table. This was Young Pioneer Zoya doing her homework. The sketch, published in the district newspaper *Moshenskoy Kolkhoznik* [Moshenskoye Collective Farm Worker], of 7 April 1935, described how Grigoriy Vasil'yevich Kruglov and his wife Fedos'ya Kapitonovna were bringing up their children. Valya, Panya, Zoya, and Boris attended the same school and all were doing well. "The school is proud to have the Kruglov children as pupils," wrote teachers S.G. Orlov and A.G. Semenov.

I am looking at a cover of a school diary, which was formerly blue but time has turned it grey. On it, it was written in a neat hand: "Z.G. Kruglova, pupil of Grade 9A," and below: "1938/39 school year." The word "excellent" was traced out in a bold hand on one of the introductory pages of the diary, beside the recorded homework assignment in biology ("From Lamarck to Darwin"). Her assignments in chemistry ("nitric oxides") and in literature ("Belinskiy's letter to Gogol'") were also rated "excellent." Zoya graduated from Grade 9 with twelve "excellent" marks.[2]

Often, on Sundays, in Zoya's native village of Moshenskoye, hundreds of young people, equipped with training rifles and respirators, marched in step to the forest showing blue on the horizon. The marches, after which paramilitary games were played, were exhilarating. Zoya was among those who took them seriously. She was a good shot, an experienced cross-country skier, and an excellent swimmer. She could orientate herself on a map, knew the Morse Code, and always faultlessly executed the orders issued by her commanders from the *Osoaviakhim* [the paramilitary Society for Assistance to Defence, Aviation, and the Chemical Industry].

Zoya Vasil'yevna Bachina, a participant in these marches, and later on an academic vice-principal of a secondary school, recalled the following incident:

"I was a soldier in the section commanded by Kruglova. We were reconnoitring when suddenly we heard the approach of the 'Blues,' both to the left and right of us. Behind us was a lake, and we had nowhere else to go. We didn't know what to do, but then and there our commander in a quiet and calm voice ordered us to hide in the reeds immediately.

"First to enter the cold water, immediately behind Kruglova, was Vanya Matveyev who loved Zoya passionately and followed her everywhere. The other girls and boys followed Vanya. However, I was procrastinating: to me, then a very young teacher, it seemed too much trouble to plunge into a lake, fully dressed, with water up to my neck. Zoya approached me, and quietly and firmly told me: 'Komsomol Bachina, do as you are told!'

"Of course, I obeyed. Soon, sub-units of the 'Blues' went by along the shore, and none of them even suspected that the 'Reds' were only twenty paces away from them."

The young people would go home in a noisy gang, their songs resounding for a long time and the silhouettes of girls and boys flashing among birch-trees until late at night. On such occasions, Zoya enjoyed breaking away from the group to go to a grove on the steep bank of the Uver'ya River, accompanied by girlfriends Nina Spartakova and Lena Almazova as well as her sister Panya. In a secluded spot, the girls shared their dreams, and then the lyrics of Zoya's favourite song "Between the Steep Shores," soared above the quiet waters.

In the summer of 1940, Zoya went to Leningrad, to take the entrance examinations to the Mining Institute. However, the unexpected happened, and hence the following scenario:

One day in August 1940, two young girls sat on the stone steps of the Lieutenant Schmidt Embankment, right by the water. One of them was crying bitterly, while the other apparently tried to calm her down, fingering the friend's heavy braids; yet, tears rolled down her cheeks too.

"Girls!" exclaimed an officer cadet attending the Frunze Higher Officer Naval School, walking past them along the Embankment: "What has happened to you?" He went down the steps toward the Neva River, and sat down beside the girls. "We failed math," said Zoya, the tearful girl with braids. Many years have passed since that time, but Anna Ivanovna Troyan (Dubrovkina), a schoolteacher in the town of Vladimir, has not forgotten the day on which she and Zoya Kruglova, candidates for admission to the Mining Institute in Leningrad, had failed their mathematics tests and ran to the Neva to have a good cry.

Here is Anna Ivanovna's account of her first encounter with Zoya Kruglova: "At the Institute I was told to go to a certain residence; I was a newcomer who didn't know the city. At the entrance I accidentally ran into a girl with long braids who apparently had been walking behind me. Though we hurt one another in the collision and were both bruised, we burst out laughing and then silently went through the door. We were assigned a dormitory full of girls. They were all chattering happily, while we sat in silence. Unexpectedly, Zoya got up and told me: 'We are meant to be friends, since fate brought us together!'

"Indeed, we became inseparable. We spent long hours studying and visiting museums together. At times, we aimlessly wandered along Leningrad embankments until it was late into the night. Everything in Leningrad delighted Zoya. She would talk for hours about the city, as if it were a living being with whom she was passionately in love."

Zoya's friendship with Anya Dubrovkina helped her to come to terms with failing her entrance examinations. She returned to her native village, and every week sent a long letter to Anya in Vladimir. The girls confided in one another and Zoya, working as chief Young Pioneer leader in her native village, reported to Anya all her successes and disappointments. On 24 April 1941 Zoya celebrated her eighteenth birthday.

At War

In the late afternoon of 22 June 1941 Zoya and her friend Lena Almazova were returning to Moshenskoye from a visit to Zoya's grandmother, the purpose of which was to cut out sun dresses for themselves. They took a shortcut through fields and meadows, chattering and singing happily. Suddenly, they ran into a group of crying women. "Haven't you heard, girls? We are at war!" Thus ended Zoya's carefree adolescence.

Similarly to many of her contemporaries, Zoya assisted in construction of defences, in receiving children evacuated from Leningrad, and in supervising students employed in harvesting. In addition, she took a first-aid course.

At Moshenskoye broadcasts of Soviet Information Bureau were awaited impatiently, but the news reports were far from cheerful. German tanks were approaching Leningrad, and enemy bombs and shells were already exploding on city squares. German strategic plans assigned a key role to the capture of Leningrad.

When the radio reported yet another air raid in Leningrad, Zoya, agitated, came to Moshenskoye District Committee of the Komsomol and placed an application on the Secretary's desk. It read as follows:

APPLICATION

"To Comrade L. Petrova, Secretary, Moshenskoye District Committee of Komsomol:

...Please send me to a Komsomol partisan detachment. I pledge to prove worthy of your trust and to serve honourably. The Nazis mustn't be left in peace, also behind their lines; our partisans mustn't let them sleep. Please don't turn me down. Dated: 14 August 1941.

Z.G. Kruglova."

Soon, Kruglova, an instructor in air and chemical defence of the Osoaviakhim's Moshenskoye District Council, was included in No. 145 "Destroyer" Battalion as a medical orderly. (At the beginning of the war, such battalions were being formed everywhere near the front lines. As a rule, they were led by line military officers or personnel of the ChEKA [colloquial name for the All-Russian Extraordinary Commission for Fighting Counter-Revolution and Sabotage].) The soldiers of Zoya's battalion protected defensive works, were on the lookout for saboteurs, and engaged enemy airborne assault landing forces. Among the participants were those who had never even handled a rifle, but all were eager to fight.

According to Timofey Andreyevich Shibanov, former commissar of the Destroyer Battalion, Kruglova quickly learned to handle captured German weapons, almost immediately mastered basic combat training, and soon received her first message of appreciation from her commander.

Once, a knocked out German bomber, looking like a black raven, overflew the outskirts of Moshenskoye with a heart-rending scream. The Battalion's patrol noticed that four dots were separating from the aircraft; these were crew members of the enemy bomber descending on their parachutes.

A group of soldiers from the Battalion were immediately sent to the drop area. When the Germans noticed them, they put their hands up. But this was only a subterfuge: after allowing the soldiers to approach them closer, the Germans began to fire their automatic weapons while attempting to break through to the edge of the forest. The Soviet soldiers were forced to go to ground. Then and there, an order given in a ringing and proud voice was heard: "Forward, comrades!"

Simultaneously, the young girl wearing a soldier's greatcoat who issued the command rushed toward the forest. The youthful, inexperienced soldiers of the Battalion followed her. Zoya Kruglova (for it was she who led the soldiers in the charge) was first to reach the forest edge. Here she almost collided with one of the Germans. They raised their arms simultaneously: the German ace, his parabellum gun, and the girl, an old rifle. She was first to fire and the airman fell.

A few days later, the brave girl stood before a staff officer of the Front (Army Group) HQ and answered his queries: "I heard that you are anxious to enlist in the regular army!" he said.

"That's correct, Comrade Major!"

"We have a difficult assignment for you in mind. You are an accomplished sportswoman, fluent in German. We plan also to give you additional training."

In this manner, Zoya became an operative of the North-Western Front. She was given 24 hours to get ready. So here was Zoya, wearing a half-length sheepskin coat, in the body of a truck, travelling along a bumpy road to Borovichi. Continuing her journey on a platform loaded with coal, she reached her destination: a school for secret agents, located in an ancient Russian settlement.

Those who trained there were never to be credited, in their service record, with participation in daring attacks or stubborn defence, even though their lives were endangered every minute and every second of their stay in an enemy camp. It was essential that, in addition to boldness and resourcefulness, they be endowed with exceptional fortitude, in order not to reveal their secret, even under all kinds of torture, in the event they were caught by enemy counterintelligence.

The training days in the ancient Russian settlement kept passing imperceptibly. Zoya's instructor Zlochevskiy was an experienced operative. Even though he was a career officer, always formal when dealing with her, during Zoya's conversations with him he reminded her of her beloved schoolteacher Ochinskaya, and she often had the urge to call him simply "Gavril Yakovlevich," instead of the regulation "Comrade Major."

A teacher evacuated from Pskov, Anya Dmitriyeva, was assigned to Kruglova's group; they were to cross over to enemy-held territory together. The girls met on their way to the intelligence school, and subsequently became friends.

Finally, one day Zlochevskiy told Zoya: "Well, Kruglova, you've been thoroughly briefed and it's time for you to go. You are obviously a hothead, so my parting words to you are: henceforward, your impulsiveness would be a handicap. You must keep cool at all times. Remember, it is most important for you not to arouse any suspicions. At first, keep a low profile...."

The Major got up and once more looked the girl over. Dressed in a winter sports outfit, the new agent was nervous, but outwardly appeared calm and confident. Only the unusual shine of her light grey eyes with bluish hue betrayed her agitation. The Major knew the reason for this agitation: only a half-hour earlier she had been designated the leader of her intelligence gathering group. The additional responsibility was an onerous burden for a 19-year-old girl.

"May I begin carrying out my mission?" asked Zoya.

"You may go now," replied Zlochevskiy, calling her by her given name for the first time. "I am sure you'll prove equal to your task."

In Enemy Camp

The whisper of the forest seemed ominous. An icy wind howled over villages and the snow-covered surface of a large lake. It was cosy and warm in the guardhouse. The German soldiers inside it hated to get out and brave the severe cold, in order to patrol the lake. Staying close to the building, the sentry didn't go to the lake, either. This is why he hadn't seen how a group of roughly twenty people, dressed in sports outfits, sped by on their cross-country skis in a single file, one behind the other. It was with this group of Soviet scouts that Kruglova's team crossed the front lines. In addition to Kruglova, the team consisted of Anya Dmitriyeva and radio operator Panya Morozova. When they left behind them an area lit up by flares and artillery shells, the girls changed into old clothes and, disguised as refugees, entered the Soshikhin District. They had yet a long way to go.

Partisans and associates who had been dropped behind enemy lines earlier helped the "refugees" to obtain a good horse and firewood. The frisky horse galloped along the snow-covered fields; however, the passengers in the cart it pulled were nervous, for even though they travelled in their native land they had to be on their guard at all times.

Soon the girls were to encounter a German lieutenant standing on the road; another German was rummaging under the hood of their car. Anya stopped the horse, and Zoya addressed the officer in fluent German: "Allow us, to pass, Mr. Officer." Surprised, he retorted in broken Russian: "Who are you? Why do you talk like a native German speaker?"

"I really am a German, Mr. Lieutenant. My name is Zoya Baiger. My father was a German. The Bolsheviks shot him in 1938, and my mother died of a broken heart. We are going to Ostrov to obtain employment and to work hard for the benefit of the Führer." Zoya's face, hitherto so sad, brightened up and her eyes were shining.

"That's good. You may pass," said the officer, mixing German and Russian. On the basis of the fabricated story, invented and developed in detail beforehand, Zoya arrived in the village of Gosteny, where Anya Dmitriyeva's father and sister lived. Anya's father hid the radio operator Morozova in his house, and Zoya made her way to the village of Vinokurovo. Such was the beginning of her new and dangerous existence.

Only a week after Kruglova's group established themselves in the district, she already managed to send intelligence on the garrison in the village of Vorontsovo as well as German airstrips, and on the behaviour of the army of occupation in general.

Still before the war, Hitler had signed a directive "On the special regime in the 'Barbarossa' area and special war measures." The soldiers of the German 18th Army and the SS-men who had flooded Pskov Region, conscientiously implemented the directive. Their presence was marked by widespread bloodshed and the black, smoking, and smouldering ruins in places where villages had once stood.

Soshikhin and Pushkinskiye Gory districts have a common boundary with Ostrov District, and the "invisible front" of the Battle for Leningrad passed there. Ostrov was an important centre, with junctions of both railways and highways along which German military supplies were transported.

In the course of her constant wanderings, Zoya were to cross the fields adjacent to the Ostrov highroad, penetrate the groves and brushwood through which the ancient road to Pushkinskiye Gory meanders like a snake, and frequent barely distinguishable forest trails. Undaunted by winter blizzards and spring thaw, Zoya would appear in the areas noted for German troop movements, at the sites of airstrip construction, and near the dispositions of punitive sub-units. *Fraulein* Baiger was to note and remember a great deal of what she had seen. Her excellent knowledge of German and self-control enabled her to gain access to German military units.

However, she found it distressing to have to listen to contemptuous remarks sent her way by ordinary Russian women. But Zoya remembered the stern admonition she had been given never to arouse enemy suspicions.

On the other hand, on some occasions she experienced moments of great joy. Once, in the late afternoon, Zoya, hugging the trunk of a mighty birch-tree, observed from a hillock how Soviet aircraft bombed an operational enemy airfield. Its construction had been finished only the day before; and she had reported this to the HQ on the previous night. So here was the result of her intelligence.

Unexpectedly, Zoya heard a young woman speaking in a quiet voice: "Why are you so happy, Baiger? After all, it seems that it is your alleged friends who are receiving their due!" Then the speaker emerged from behind some brushwood, a smile on her pale face. She appeared to be very pleased with the performance of Soviet pilots. After regaining her composure, Zoya retorted angrily: "It's you who appears to be happy; without a doubt you're a partisan."

"I am happy, though I am not a partisan. Are you going to report me? Well, if so, come with me. You don't want to? How strange!" It was dangerous to remain in the grove any longer, and Zoya decided to leave. The stranger told her at parting: "I've heard bad things about you, but today I saw how overjoyed you were to see our aircraft at work. Let's get acquainted, Baiger. I am from Ostrov and my name is Filippova. Drop in on me when you are in town. The Germans also call me *Fraulein*."

"All right!" replied Zoya, and shook the hand extended to her. Their growing sense of affinity caused them to throw caution to the wind. However, both Kruglova and Filippova, an Ostrov underground member who was returning from Vorontsovo after a rendez-vous with a partisan messenger, proved justified in trusting their intuition. Zoya had heard about the Ostrov underground lead by Klava Nazarova, while still training in her intelligence school. She knew that Nazarova's closest associates were Lyudmila Filippova, an employee of the Komsomol District Committee, and three young men who had graduated from the same secondary school in 1941: Oleg Serebrennikov, Leva Sudakov, and Sasha Mitrofanov. Kruglova was aware of some of their exploits, but she had not been given permission to establish contact with them, and so far she avoided the town.

In May 1942 Zoya's team suffered a misfortune: their radio mal-functioned. They counted on nearby partisans to make the necessary repairs; the radio operator went away to make contact with them, but failed to come back. On the other hand, both Zoya and Anya had accumulated important intelligence. After consulting her friends, Zoya decided to cross over to Soviet-held territory to obtain further instructions.

* * *

Meanwhile, harassed by partisans, the Germans increased their vigilance, and in particular watched closely the railway section between Sushchevo and Chikhachevo. Zoya attempted to cross the tracks in this area, which was out of bounds for the local population. She was apprehended by a group of policemen, one of whom took her to the nearest kommandatura. On the way, she chose an appropriate moment to jump into a clump of bushes. A shot rang out and a bullet buzzed over her head. She had to find another way of crossing the front lines.

Barefooted and hungry, she made her way through a swamp, through lowland water and hillocks covered with sickly pines, and again water, rusty and cold. She had nowhere to sit down to rest, and nowhere to warm herself. Her feet covered with scabs and bruises and her face gaunt, not for a moment was she discouraged and lost her determination to persevere in her struggle.

The fog-covered swamp, stretching for many kilometres, seemed uninhabited, but the sensitive ear of a partisan sentry picked up a vague sound; someone slowly made his way to their camp. The sentry awakened his comrades, and they noiselessly disappeared into the fog. In a few minutes, a woman in rags confronted the partisan patrol. She refused to answer questions put to her and demanded to be taken to the commander. "Again, the vile creatures sent us a spy; a punitive detachment will likely follow in her tracks," a member of the patrol said in an angry voice. "Why pussyfoot with her?"

"I agree!" another one joined in. However, the third one rushed toward the arrested woman with a cry: "Zoya!" His name was Volod'ya Verkh and he recognized in her a classmate from their native village. In about twenty-four hours, Zoya was escorted to her unit. Here, a decoration, the Medal for Bravery, awaited her.

Stronger Than Death

How wonderful it was to be home on leave! After her long absence and the trials she had undergone, her parents' cottage by the Uver'ya River, and the school surrounded by trees with jackdaw nests, had become even dearer to her than before. Nevertheless, mindful of the horrors of German occupation, she decided to return to her unit as soon as possible.

Having cut short her stay at home, she again stood before her commander, waiting to be assigned yet another mission.

"Good," said the Colonel; "you'll be dropped from an aircraft in a very important area in Pskov Region, and we have yet to assign you a radio operator. In the meantime, you'll be given an additional briefing."

Soon an aircraft carrying Zoya and Zinaida Boykova, the new radio operator, whose call sign was "Fantasy," landed in the Partisan Territory in the village of Zaluch'ye, to the south of Polisto Lake in Pskov Region. The aircraft, on its way back to the "Mainland," carried Zoya's letter to her family:

"Please don't worry about me. I am bound to surmount all the difficulties, as I did in the past. You'll be my lodestar. I pledge to you that I'll carry out the orders of my beloved Fatherland.... I feel very well; I have an iron constitution. The weather here is glorious.... When you consider the circumstances in which our young people's youth is slipping away, you hate the vile creatures even more. I don't know whether I'll live to see the restoration of the happy life we lived before the war, but I'll do my best to make it possible for my friends and comrades."

The Germans sent tanks, aircraft, and entire divisions to the Partisan Territory. The commander of a partisan regiment that covered the evacuation of wagon trains loaded with wounded partisans detailed twelve men armed with submachine guns to the escort of Kruglova's group, even though he was short of personnel himself. They had to make their way to the swamp, and then Zoya was led by several guides across the unstable moss and boggy undergrowth.

One night, someone knocked on the window of Anya Dmitriyeva's house at Gosteny. Anya was awake. In the evening, when she was returning home from her regular trip to the airfield, a policeman kept following her. He was drunk, but nevertheless behaved suspiciously; he didn't pester her, as usual, with his compliments, but instead kept asking questions about herself and hinted that he had contacts with partisans. When she heard a knock, Anya at first became frightened; then she quickly regained self-control, threw a half-length sheepskin coat over her bare shoulders, and went out onto the porch.

Two young lads stood in front of her. One of them, a short and sturdy fellow, came up close and said quietly: "Greetings from Uncle Grisha."

"I am glad you've come, and I appreciate the greetings you bring." These phrases were passwords. In a minute, the sturdy fellow (it was the scout Alferov) was sitting behind the table in the kitchen, eating a cold cabbage soup with gusto in the dark. Just before leaving at dawn, he warned her that some acquaintances would pay her a visit in two weeks.

The two weeks dragged on and on. Finally, on a dark night just like the one on which Alferov came, Zoya arrived and the girls hugged and kissed one another. Again, they were reunited!

Soon an order came from the HQ instructing Baiger and Boykova to go to Ostrov, in order to establish themselves there as legal residents. The German army suffered heavy losses in the vicinity of Leningrad and reinforcements were being sent there through Ostrov and Pskov. Consequently, Soviet military authorities required accurate data on the Ostrov lines of communication.

Zinaida Boykova then wrote a letter to her loved ones in Ostrov (her brother and sister were not on the police list of suspects), telling them that she had returned to Pskov Region with a German officer as his mistress, but he abandoned her. A girlfriend persuaded her not to hide all this from her family and to return home. When she was reunited with her father, she told him the truth.

After receiving their passports, the girls found jobs: Boykova as a cleaning woman in a military unit and Kruglova as a clerk in an employment agency.[3] It proved difficult for them to communicate with their HQ. They had to fling out their antenna onto the roof and lift it on a pole, which was very risky. All the same, in November 1942 they managed to transmit four radiograms containing important data about the locations of large ammunition dumps, new aircraft on the Ostrov airfield, and movements of military units along the Kiev Highway.[4]

The underground activists were hardly idle either. With each day, the Nazi authorities and Sasse, commandant of the 822nd Field Kommandatura, became convinced more and more that they were dealing with a Resistance organization. Uniformed police and detectives did everything they could to track down members of the underground, but failed to do so for some time. However, eventually they managed to arrest a few individuals, having come by the pertinent information by accident.

In the early morning of 15 December 1942, the inhabitants of Ostrov were herded into the market square to witness an execution [of several local members of the Resistance] and were told the names of the prisoners who had been condemned to death by hanging "for collaborating with Party members, partisans, and bandits, as well as for resisting the new regime."

The proud and unrepentant Resistance leader Klava Nazarova stood in the body of a truck, listening to the monotone in which the sentence was read; her associate Nyura Ivanova huddled up close to her, apprehensively glancing at the gallows hewed out from fresh pine logs. When the executioners approached them, Klava, in a ringing voice, shouted to the crowd: "Good-bye, friends! Good-bye, my dear town!" The enemy soldiers attempted to prevent her from speaking, but the final words of the heroine reached the people: "The Red Army will come. We are bound to win!"

At a certain distance from the crowd, a well-dressed young woman stood on a hillock. She hid her face in a soft, downy kerchief. When Klava's final words resounded in the frosty air, the girl slumped for a moment, but straightened herself up immediately after she had heard footsteps behind her. "Are you enjoying it, beautiful? All of you will end up like this," a German officer told her in Russian. He looked her over impudently from head to foot, letting out a hiccup. "It won't happen to me, Mr. Lieutenant," replied the girl in German.

"Forgive me, *Fraulein*."

"*Fraulein* Baiger," the stranger said proudly. She removed the kerchief from her head, and contemptuously looked at the drunk lieutenant. "Without a doubt, you're new here; otherwise, I would have met you at the Kommandatura."

"Again that Baiger caught an officer," an elderly woman, a bystander, remarked with hostility. "Especially on a day like today. Obviously, she is new to this town."

In the evening Baiger accompanied the love-sick lieutenant to the train station; he was catching up with his unit on its way to the Leningrad Front. Only a half an hour later the girl was sitting in her room, writing by the light of a kerosene lamp. How truly surprised would have been the woman who had spoken with such hostility about Zoya in the morning, in the square, if she had seen what Baiger had written! Zoya Baiger, the German, was composing a cipher message about Nazi tank troop movements, which she extracted from documents she had found in the lieutenant's map case.

It was becoming more and more dangerous for her to operate in

Ostrov. After executing Klava Nazarova, the Gestapo kept tracking down her comrades. "I feel as if I were inside a stone sack, in Ostrov," complained Zoya to Anya on one occasion when they met. Soon she noticed that she was placed under surveillance. The director of her agency sent her to a military unit needlessly. There she was followed by a "civilian," in whom Zoya recognized an officer from the Kommandatura.[5]

By the time she decided to go away, it was too late. She barely managed, after she noticed a Gestapo vehicle parked in front of her building, to swallow a note she had received from one of her assistants.

During her first interrogation, Zoya was not beaten and nobody even shouted at her. The investigator stated that he respected her for her daring, and promised to spare her life in exchange for the betrayal of her comrades. "Be compliant, Kruglova; we already know everything."

"There is nothing to be compliant about, Mr. Lieutenant. I am not in the least guilty. You are confused: I am not Kruglova but Baiger."

The contest in staying power lasted for a few days. The girl from Moshenskoye had more of it than this master of bloodletting from the vicinity of Pillau did. During one of the interrogations, he screamed at her: "I'll make you talk, you Russian wench!" Then he rushed at Zoya like a wild animal and started hitting her with whatever he had at hand. She blacked out. When Zoya regained consciousness, she saw the Gestapo man, who looked like a vulture, bending over her. "Well, are you going to tell me now who you really are?"

"Zoya Baiger; I already told you. Baiger," replied the girl quietly. Her eyes had acquired a dry shine. There was so much hate in them that the interrogator involuntarily screamed: "Take her to her cell!"

She guessed from the questions put to her that her team was betrayed by a secret enemy at the airfield (she had guessed correctly, as was confirmed after the war). Zoya started to talk about herself, but her version totally confused the investigator. Boykova, who had been arrested as well, also stuck to this version during her interrogation, but on the whole she withstood beatings and tortures with less fortitude than Kruglova did.

The VIPs in the Gestapo became interested in the Baiger case. As a result, in the spring of 1943 she was transferred to the death camp at Pskov. On the other hand, Boykova was almost immediately sent to Germany, to a Düsseldorf jail.

Almost nothing is known about Kruglova's stay at the death camp. Her friends considered her to be doomed when she suddenly escaped from Gestapo clutches. Together with Nina Berezhito (an agent left behind in Pskov Region in 1941), Zoya made a daring escape from the camp. The girls had persuaded their guard to let them out and to accompany them to the Velikaya River, where they wished to rinse out their laundry. On the river bank, they wrested a submachine gun away from the guard, and threw themselves into the river.

Afterwards, Zoya was to surface again; she was tracked down to a partisan brigade. From there Zoya, accompanied by a guide — a young woman partisan — made her way to the front lines via Novorzhev District. But a detachment of "false partisans" unexpectedly entered the village in which the girls stopped for a rest; it was led by an experienced agent provocateur Martynovskiy. Zoya was asleep when her inexperienced guide confided in Martynovskiy that she and Zoya were partisans, too. During the night the "partisans" revealed their true identity by staging executions in the village and robbing its population. Captured, Zoya was sent to Ostrov under a reinforced escort.

A truck sped through a field, jumping up like a ball on the pot-holes. Zoya, lying on her back in the body of the truck, looked at the starry sky and for the first time cried in the presence of the enemy. She was vexed that she had been caught in such an absurd fashion. Beyond the brushwood flashing along the sides of the road, she could guess the outlines of the sleeping forest. She had such an urge to make a dash for the forest and to hide there from her escorts!

Zoya was incarcerated in the same jail as before. The pedantic warden placed her in the same cell. She was interrogated less but beaten more often than during her first arrest.

Her tortured body hurt terribly; she had the urge to scream to the top of her voice with pain. However, she knew her enemies must not hear her moan, and they mustn't see suffering in her face. Zoya closed her eyes. Dawn was breaking. She heard the clanging of bolts; a group of prisoners were going out to their outside jobs under escort. Overcoming a terrible dizziness, the girl raised herself to the window. Then the ringing sound of her singing escaped the cell: "Go, our locomotive, full speed ahead!"

"This crazy Baiger is at it again," mumbled her guard, huddling himself up as if expecting a blow. Three German soldiers ran toward Zoya's cell.

Zoya's Last Letter

On 1 September Zoya learned that she will be executed shortly. The colonel from Pskov Gestapo who was present at her interrogation had forgotten that she understood German well, and on departing flung at her torturers: "Finish with Baiger!"

Only miracle could save her now, and she didn't believe in miracles. She had an urge to send a letter home and she managed to do it. The Germans often required middle-aged women sentenced to a short-term imprisonment to work at the local saw-mill. One day, one of them said to Dusya Demidova who was employed as a cleaning woman at the mill: "Don't look behind you; I know you're Demidova. After I am gone, pick up my note; Zoya had asked me to pass it onto your sister Nyura."

Zoya had often seen Nyura Demidova at parties. The young women liked each other; twice they walked home together. Nyura openly cursed the army of occupation and maintained that she wasn't afraid of Zoya reporting her to the authorities, despite Zoya's unsavoury reputation. Zoya didn't reveal her true identity to Nyura, while considering the latter her last recourse. Passing the note amounted to taking advantage of this "last recourse." Zoya's note contained the following message: "Please bring me some warm, cooked potatoes. I would like to have something good to eat before I die." When Zoya became convinced that the note had reached its destination, she sent her final message out of the prison by the same route. Her letter read as follows:

"Hello, my dear Mom and Dad and my dear sisters, Valechka, Panechka, and Shura, as well as my dear brother Borechka. I am writing to you, my dear ones, from prison for the last time. You'll receive this letter after I am gone.

"My dear ones, an entire year has passed since you heard from me; you had no news from me at all since then. All this time I was on the move, but I haven't forgotten you. I was arrested in February and spent two and a half months in a solitary, in jail. Every day I expected to be shot. Mom, I had a very hard time, but I withstood everything. I was sent to a camp in Pskov, where I spent two months, and then I ran away and crossed over to our territory. I was sent on another mission, and I am again incarcerated in the same jail; I am spending the second month here already. I was beaten with sticks about the head. I am expecting to be shot; I no longer think about the future, even though I long to live a bit longer so, in order to be re-united with you, my dear ones, give you an affectionate hug, and sob out all my grief on your breast, my dear Mom. After all, if I haven't been caught the second time, I would have come home in September. But apparently it was fated to happen, and I am not at all protesting it. I've discharged my duty. My dear ones, be proud that I had never dishonoured you nor myself. I am going to die, but not in vain.

"Mom, you in particular, should not upset yourself over me; don't cry. I would like to comfort you, but I am very far from you, behind iron bars and strong walls. I often sing in the Jail and the entire Jail listens to me. Here is a song about me and my sad end:

> Don't cry, don't cry, my dear,
> Don't be sad, my old mother.
> We'll smash Nazi vile creatures,
> At home again we'll gather.
>
> But she died; she didn't return
> From her Ostrov Jail cell.
> She was executed one night
> By the Ostrov Jail wall.

"My dear ones, you will be told everything about me by my acquaintances, provided these girls survive. I beg you once more: don't cry, don't be sad. Remember me for the last time to Aunt Liza, Uncle Vanya, Lena Almazova, and to all my girlfriends, relatives, and acquaintances.

"Lots of love and kisses to you.

"Good-bye, forever.

"My body will lie in the town of Ostrov, behind the Jail, beside the road. Dear Mom, I'll be wearing my faded black woollen dress, the knitted red sweater you had bought for me, and Russian-style boots.

"Your daughter Zoya.

"Good-bye, good-bye."

On 9 September 1943, at dawn, a covered truck drove through the Jail gate. Anastasiya Ivanovna Serebrennikova, the mother of Oleg Serebrennikov, who stood beside the gate all night with a message, heard the voice of Mila Filippova and saw Sasha Mitrofanov. Anastasiya Ivanovna ran behind the truck until it disappeared from view beyond the turn of the road. Three days later, the Mayor's secretary Kazantsev secretly showed the Order for the Execution to Serebrennikova. Five surnames were mentioned in the Order: Filippova, Sudakov, Serebrennikov, Mitrofanov, and Kruglova-Baiger.

In the summer of 1944, the Pskov Region, already scorched by conflagration of the war, experienced a new Soviet offensive. Abandoning the grim partisan localities and consumed by fury, the enemy troops set fire to everything they previously had no time to destroy. They turned the towns of Ostrov, Idritsa, and Pushinskiye Gory into smouldering ruins. Pustoshka and many other towns and villages were also reduced to ashes.

The streets along which Soviet soldiers marched were almost completely deserted. A portion of the population of Pskov languished in captivity, and some still remained in the woods, in partisan detachments. However, many died at the hands of executioners, on the gallows and in jails.

The marching Soviet soldiers were silent, moved by the emaciated faces of old men and women. They listened to stories of Nazi atrocities, and memorized the names of heroes of the Resistance. The toil-worn hands of the soldiers squeezed their submachine guns tightly; the regiments kept shortening their halts.

When the soldiers were leaving Ostrov for Riga,[6] they were carrying copies of Zoya's last letter. Written with blood, the letter called for revenge and inspired to victory.

Nevertheless, the exploits of Zoya, an ordinary Russian girl from the village of Moshenskoye, would have been forgotten but for the efforts of her friends. Among those who helped to piece the pertinent events together, after the lapse of more than fifteen years, were Anya Dmitriyeva, Zoya's comrade-in-arms; Zoya's childhood friends; and many other Soviet people.

On the basis of the application submitted by the Military Council of the Leningrad Military District, the Supreme Soviet of the USSR conferred the Order of Patriotic War I Class on Zoya Grigor'yevna Kruglova posthumously. On 9 May 1959 the Order was presented as a memento to Fedos'ya Kapitonovna, Zoya's mother. The war had cost this remarkable woman her husband, one son, and one daughter.

The German authorities purposely kept secret the site of the execution, where Kruglova and four leaders of the Ostrov underground were buried. In the fall of 1959, some of the Komsomols of the town managed to unravel the mystery. Here is how it happened.

Among the local inhabitants, present at the execution, was a village elder named Aleksey Petrov. On 9 September 1943 he barged into a peasant house, demanding some home-brew. After emptying a second glass, he confessed: "I witnessed the execution of the Ostrov Komsomols. I recognized the son of Ivan Mitrofanov. The girls were lying on the ground, while the lads dug the common grave."

The collaborator Petrov was arrested after the war; he died soon after he had served his sentence. When the search for the location of the common grave began, Veronika Zhatova, a former classmate of Oleg Serebrennikov, suggested that Petrov could have revealed the location to somebody before he died. Zhatova persevered in making her inquiries; finally, after some hesitation the elder's niece revealed what she had learned from her uncle. The young patriots were shot on the 7th versta [versta = 3,500 feet] from the town, in the brushwood a little to one side of the Ostrov — Palkino Highway.

On a gloomy day in September 1959, the inhabitants of the ancient town accompanied the remains of the five young people to their final resting place. Thousands crowded into the central town square, carrying the portraits of Zoya, Mila, Oleg, Leva, and Sasha, which Young Pioneers had adorned with fresh flowers. Many tears were shed, many moving speeches were given, and the town demonstrated how proud it was of its loyal sons and daughters. Only those who have struck a responsive, deep chord in people's hearts are remembered in this manner.

NOTES

1.   *Tayna Zoi Kruglovoy*. Leningrad: Lenizdat, 1962, 72pp.

2.   Zoya Kruglova was born on 24 April 1923 in the village of Moshenskoye of Novgorod Region. See Minayeva, *et al.*, eds., *Srazhalas*, p. 25.

3.   At first she was entrusted by the German authorities with matters of secondary importance, but when they established that she carried out her duties with great enthusiasm and genuine German pedantry, Zoya was granted a pass giving her unrestricted freedom of movement in the territory of the local garrison, and she was often employed as an interpreter. In the late evening she would meet Boykova at a secret address and passed intelligence data to her for transmission to military authorities of the North-Western Front. See *Na zemle Novgorodskoy. Ocherki iz istorii Novgorodskoy oblasti* [In the Land of Novgorod: Sketches on the History of Novgorod Region], V.N. Bazovskiy, *et al.*, eds. (Leningrad: Lenizdat, 1970), p. 267.

4.   As a result, Soviet bombers destroyed two ammunition dumps, one troop train, and the Ostrov airfield.

5.   Boykova argued they should go away to a partisan unit, since it was becoming very difficult to live in the enemy camp, despised by one's own people. But Zoya assured her that it was their duty to remain at their posts.

6.   *Moshenskoye kolkhoznik* [Moshenskoye Collective Farm Worker], the district newspaper, published in 1944 an article by war correspondents Majors A. Chakovskiy and M. Semenov, entitled "Posledneye pis'mo [The Last Letter]," about Zoya's exploit. They obtained the text of the letter from one of Zoya's friends residing in Riga, after the expulsion of German troops from that city.

SCHEDULED TO APPEAR IN 1998

WOMEN IN WAR AND RESISTANCE:
SELECTED BIOGRAPHIES OF SOVIET WOMEN SOLDIERS
by Kazimiera J. Cottam

(A collection consisting of 100 original mini-biographies. Includes thirty-five biographies of bomber, fighter, and ground attack pilots and navigators, and of one radio-operator/air gunner, in addition to other military personnel, partisans and secret agents.)

ORDERING INFORMATION

Bookstores and Libraries:
    In Canada and the USA: 1-888-780-4125
For Individuals:
    In Canada and the USA: 1-888-780-4125
or, send pre-paid order, plus $3.50, along with your name and address to:

NEW MILITARY PUBLISHING
83-21 Midland Crescent
Nepean, ON K2H 8P6 CANADA